Issues

GENERAL

Gende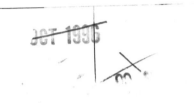

Other Books in This Series

John Darling and
Anthony Glendinning

Gender Matters in Schools

Pupils and Teachers

CASSELL

Cassell

Wellington House 215 Park Avenue South
125 Strand New York
London WC2R 0BB NY 10003

First published 1996

British Library Cataloguing-in-Publication Data
A catalogue record for this book is available from the
British Library.

ISBN 0–304–32803–0 (hardback)
      0–304–32805–7 (paperback)

Typeset by Action Typesetting Limited, Gloucester
Printed and bound in Great Britain by Redwood Books,
Trowbridge, Wiltshire

Contents

Foreword: the purpose of this series

The educational scene is changing rapidly. This change is being caused by a complexity of factors which includes a re-examination of present educational provision against a background of changing social and economic policies, new forms of testing and assessment, a National Curriculum, and local management of schools with more participation by parents.

As the educational process is concerned with every aspect of our lives and our society both now and for the future, it is of vital importance that all teachers, teachers in training, administrators and educational policy-makers should be aware and informed on current issues in education.

This series of books is thus designed to inform on current issues, to look at emerging ones, and to give an authoritative overview which will be of immense help to all those involved in the education process.

Philip Hills
Cambridge

Acknowledgements

We appreciate the co-operation of TVEI Grampian, and particularly the support of Ann Summers and Ruth Warren. Excellent secretarial assistance was provided by Margaret Sinclair.

We are grateful for permission to use material from the following sources:

Strathclyde Regional Council Education Department (1988) *Sex Equality in the Education Service*, SRC, Glasgow.

Darling, J. (1986) 'Child-centred, gender-centred: a criticism of progressive educational theory from Rousseau to Plowden', *Oxford Review of Education*, 12(1). Carfax Publishing, Abingdon, Oxfordshire.

Darling, J. (1992) 'The best man for the job: women teachers, promotion, and the Strathclyde research', *Scottish Educational Review*, 24(1).

Introduction

In 1842 a schoolteacher called Max Stirner argued that instead of possessing our own ideas, we are in fact ourselves possessed by ideas we have internalized from dominant elements in society. He introduced the phrase 'wheels in the head' to refer to beliefs which we have acquired without any process of choice, decision, deliberation, or conscious adoption. Amongst these are our ideas of what follows from the fact that we are one sex rather than the other. Today, however, many people are engaged in unpacking these assumptions, and subjecting them to critical scrutiny and debate.

In the past, answers to questions about the education and role of females and males, assuming they have even been articulated, have too often been of the common-sense type; that is to say they have not been critically examined. This is a point which goes beyond mere theoretical concern, for the phenomenon is quite noticeable in the pronouncements of those who have influenced educational policy.

In 1959 a major influence on educational thinking was the Crowther Report which argued that the way ahead was to make the curriculum clearly relevant to pupils' future lives and livelihoods. But the practical import of this vocationalism would, it seems, be significantly affected by the pupil's sex. The educational potential of 'machinery' seemed to Crowther's committee as exciting then as information technology does to many educationists today. A vocational interest in machinery, however, was not seen as universal: girls' interests were different, but had their own potential.

The passionate interest that many girls feel in living things can be as strong an educational incentive as the love of machines. It is not for nothing that biology is the main science taught to girls, as physics and chemistry are to boys. The same forces, whether innate or social does not matter, probably determine the fact that girls show a more conscious and avowed interest in personal relations than boys do.   (Crowther Committee, 1959, p. 112)

Four years later, the Newsom report on the education of 'average and less than average' pupils continued in the same vein, confident that its pronouncements would be accepted as eminently good sense.

Many of our boys are going to work with their hands, whether in skilled or unskilled jobs. Many of them already own a bicycle and soon after they leave school may hope to own a motor bike; car engines, transistor radios, tape recorders, are all within their range of everyday interests. In not so many years' time, as young married men, they will very likely be busy with domestic power tools and do-it-yourself kits, with home decorating and the building of garden sheds and garages.

(Newsom Committee, 1963, p. 36)

Courses should involve tools, 'the handling and working of various types of materials', and (again) machinery. According to the report, courses should be designed with an eye on the nature of local industries to underline their vocational value.

In case all this practical relevance sounds rather mundane, it should be pointed out that the argument is not beyond taking a turn towards the romantic.

A boy is usually excited by the prospect of a science course. What is it that appeals to him? He experiences a sense of wonder and a sense of power. The growth of wheat, the birth of a lamb, the movement of clouds put him in awe of nature; the locomotive and telephone he sees as man's response; the switch and the throttle are his magic wands. If he cannot produce a sunset he can change the colour in his test tube.   (Newsom Committee, 1963, p. 142)

2

But girls are not to be left out!

> The girl may come to the science lesson with a less eager curiosity
> than the boy, but she too will need to feel at home with machinery
> and will be subject to the prestige which science has in the world.
> In the future she may earn her living in as scientific an occupation
> as the boy. Whether science to her is friend or enemy she will be
> better equipped by having some inkling [*sic*] of its nature.
>
> (Newsom Committee, 1963, p. 142)

If some of these points are advanced with careful qualification, there is no hesitation in identifying one concern which is
apparently universal in girls.

> For all girls ... there is a group of interests relating to what many,
> perhaps most of them, would regard as their most important voca-
> tional concern, marriage. It is true that at the age of fourteen and
> fifteen, this may appear chiefly as preoccupation with personal
> appearance and boy friends, but many girls are ready to respond
> to work relating to the wider aspects of homemaking and family
> life and the care and upbringing of children.
>
> (Newsom Committee, 1963, p. 37)

In articulating gender roles in this kind of way, committees
fail to examine their own assumptions about the appropriate-
ness of females and males following different curricula and
different life patterns. Whether consciously or otherwise, such
reports effectively endorse what are gendered 'tracks' to be
followed by young people through the process of schooling
and into future adult life.

What is striking here is that this stereotyping is not
produced by Neanderthal chauvinists, but by people who are
often described half-mockingly as the 'great and the good'.
Their reports are self-consciously enlightened and well-
meaning. Liberal sentiment is particularly abundant in the
Plowden Report, about which we will have more to say in a
later chapter. Here it will be enough to draw attention to a
scenario described by the head of a village school and which is

3

reproduced approvingly in the committee's report. What started with the acquisition of some frog-spawn grew into a major study of the ecology of water.

> After discussion it was decided that plastic would hold water and having some big plastic bags the boys dug a hole and made a very satisfactory pond which lasted until the summer holidays. This gave them the chance of seeing the final development into frogs and the comparison of indoor and outdoor growth. Discussions arose naturally on stagnant water, fresh water, drinking water and flowing water...
> After this a girl brought a jar of water from the football field to show me that it was not fit to drink although it was always used for the players' tea. Then the boys wanted to find out if the rain water running down the bank contained any debris.
>
> [Plowden Committee, 1967, p. 243]

One critic quite reasonably enquires whether there were no girls who were interested in the running water (Byrne, 1978, p. 45). But it is not just females of primary-school age who are seen as lacking in this kind of curiosity. It has also been pointed out that the Robbins Report (1963), which endorsed the expansion of higher education, believed that women had 'naturally' less interest in proceeding to research after their first degree (Sutherland, 1981, p. 177).

Stereotyping of this kind is endemic in our culture. The expectation that men should be strong and active, while women are weak and passive is apparent to children from an early age. 'Page 3 girls' (and countless other aspects of contemporary culture) are essentially a continuation of this theme, one which many male youngsters learn to see as the norm. When Clare Short introduced her Indecent Displays Bill in Parliament in response to this sort of material, she was overwhelmed by the volume of letters of support from women. One letter asks two telling questions:

> How can a little boy be expected to grow up believing people are people regardless of genitalia, with equal rights and potentials,

when he is constantly confronted with the bizarre fact that the most important thing about women is that they have breasts? How can a little girl be expected to have the same hopes and expectations as her brother – aspire to be an engineer or a bank manager or a computer programmer – when she is constantly presented with role models of 'ideal women' whose mission in life is to please men?

(Short, 1991, p. 84)

Traditional male and female stereotypes have long been a feature of reading material used in school classrooms. Lobban (1974) examined 179 stories in six reading schemes, and found twice as many heroes as heroines. Boys in the stories were more likely to take the lead, learn new skills, show initiative and be successful. Mothers in the stories were invariably shown as exclusively concerned with domestic activity.

Educational publishers today are in general much more sensitive to these matters, not necessarily because of any commitment to equal opportunities, but because in a changing social climate, the buyers of books and other materials (i.e. schools and local education authorities) do make such formal commitments to equal opportunities policies. Indicative of this heightened awareness is the following collection of statements which are now declared by publishers as unacceptable:

The ancient Egyptians allowed women considerable control over property.

The American colonists brought their wives and children to the New World.

Women were given the vote after the First World War.

Marie Curie did what few people – men or women – could do.

Throughout this region the prairie farmer was concerned about the price of his wheat.

Older material which has not been through the hands of this

5

type of editor, however, often continues in use, not least because of the financial constraints under which schools operate. And not all publishers are equally particular. Jerome Bruner's anthropology-oriented integrated studies course is still marketed as MACOS (Man: A Course of Study).

The use of the generic 'he' and 'his' is still widespread. This may be objected to because of its tendency to marginalize girls or make them less visible. In some cases, however, it can also be a cause of genuine confusion. Does the examiner who set the following question want pupils to confine themselves to male characters or not?

> Choose a character who is in conflict with himself or with some other character in the play.

Encouragingly, the Scottish Examination Board has scrutinized its own 1993 examination papers for sexist language, gender imbalance and stereotyping, and it concludes that in the majority of subjects there is little or no evidence of gender bias, although this is not universal. It notes, for example, that girls in science questions tended to be contextualized in the home. The report asks: 'Is it the function of examinations to reflect society or to be an instrument of change within society?' (SEB, 1995, p. 4). Clearly there is a genuine tension here. There are, after all, good educational reasons for setting examination questions (and, of course, learning material generally) in a 'realistic' or conventional context. However, although gender bias in assessment is a serious concern, the idea that examination questions can change society may seem rather optimistic.

It is understandable that there has been some scepticism about the preoccupation with getting the cosmetics of language put right. Yet it is entirely likely that sexist language does help to confirm, if not create, stereotyped pictures in the minds of readers and listeners. Such language also reveals much about the pictures in the mind of the person making the utterance. Most alarming is the following statement from the government minister responsible for education in Scotland: 'if a parent is concerned, he [sic] should see the headmaster and the masters in the school concerned' (Douglas-Hamilton, 1993). Inevitably, one wonders how far the minister's understanding of the schools under his jurisdiction is coloured by his own experience of single-sex, public school education.

The world we will be talking about in this book is one in which schools have both male and female teachers. We shall explore how far the situation has changed and how far it has remained constant both for pupils and for their teachers. In the 1860s needlework was added to the 'three Rs' for girls only in what was roughly the equivalent of today's National Curriculum. More than a hundred years later, in 1974 (the year before the Sex Discrimination Act) the Inspectorate found that in Scottish primary schools the teaching of needlework to girls was still 'a significant planned difference in the curriculum of boys and girls' (HMI, 1975, p. 8). Today, deliberate differentiation by gender has stopped. But do more fundamental inequities continue?

This book is designed to start with a consideration of theory, history, and broad social context, and then to become increasingly focused on the empirical and the particular, finishing with a discussion of findings based on a local study of seven secondary schools in one region of Scotland. Chapter 1 offers an important reminder. The debate about women's role in society and its relationship to education has not only been of recent concern: the subject has a history.

1 A woman's place: the early critics

From Plato onwards there has been discussion about the rightful place of women in society, by men, and much less visibly by women. Yet, exactly because of the position of women in Western societies throughout much of this period, women have 'a history of their own' which has, until recently, gone largely unrecognized. Anderson and Zinsser's (1990) extensive narrative of women's place in European society from pre-history up to the present time makes this strikingly clear. Their starting point is that there has always been a disparity between the image of women presented by men and women's own experience. Included in this disparity has been the myth that women have no history, or at least, that there is little worthy of inclusion in the historical record. Anderson and Zinsser, in re-writing a history of European women, 'reluctantly' conclude that for much of this time gender has been the key factor in shaping the lives of women; women have traditionally been viewed first as women, as a separate class. By contrast, men have been seen as divided by social position, nation, and the era in which they lived their lives.

Another key factor has been that, until very recently, all women have been defined by their relationship to men: even those women who joined religious orders were seen as 'brides of Christ'. Women's primary role has been the care of the home and the family, but women's work, whether inside the home or outside, has traditionally been regarded as of less value and of lower status than that of men, and has brought fewer rewards. European women's lives have therefore been consistently limited by restrictions on opportunities and resources. And even for those women who have managed to avoid such restrictions, a further constraining factor, perhaps the most powerful and the most resistant to change, has been:

> European culture's largely negative views of women. Considered innately flawed, less valuable, and thus inferior to men, all women were supposed to be subordinate to men. This subordination seemed part of the natural order.
>
> (Anderson and Zinsser, 1990, p. xvii)

Although women occupied a subordinate position, with limits and restrictions on their lives, many found value in their reproductive and nuturing role, and in identifying with traditions which saw these roles in positive terms. However,

> Most did not rebel, or their rebellion left no traces in the historical record. For the ideology of women's inferiority was so deeply integrated into the fabric of both women's and men's lives that few questioned it.   (Anderson and Zinsser, 1990, p. xvii)

That some individuals were able to see beyond their culture's attitudes, however, is clearly shown by the writings of women like Mary Wollstonecraft in the eighteenth century. But if we are to understand Mary Wollstonecraft's arguments in defence of women, we must consider not just what was said about the position of women at the time, but also what was said about the position of men.

All men are equal. This idea influenced those who framed the American constitution. It was also the inspiration behind the storming of the Bastille. Philosophers had long maintained that what distinguished man from beast was man's ability to reason. In the second half of the eighteenth century it was declared that since all men possessed the faculty of reason, all men were equal. Any form of society, therefore, which failed to reflect this equality (and most societies certainly fell into this class) was indefensible and ought not to be tolerated. Old hierarchical social systems had to give way: hence the French Revolution, and the democratic spirit of the newly independent United States.

Like many important ideas, Mary Wollstonecraft's was simplicity itself. She took the argument about the rights of man and applied it to the situation of women. Women were also, she maintained, endowed with the faculty of reason. Therefore men and women were equal. Therefore a social structure which cast one sex in an inferior position would have to be changed. Wollstonecraft's *Vindication of the Rights of Woman*, published in 1792, while not the first, is the most celebrated early critique of gender privilege. In particular, it shows how the issue of education is intertwined with questions about human society and human nature.

In England after the French Revolution, to argue for the rights of man was to be seen as subversive; to argue for the rights of women was to invite derision. In the preceding decades many authors had addressed the question of the position of women in society, with most putting forward views which were marked by varying degrees of conservatism. Here we will consider the views of three male authors who were explicitly attacked by Wollstonecraft in *Vindication of the Rights of Woman*: John Gregory, James Fordyce, and Jean-Jacques Rousseau, writing in Edinburgh, London, and France respectively. Wollstonecraft was concerned to criticize a literature which both supported the subordinate position of women, and encouraged women to accept their rightful and inevitable position in society, as 'the toy of a man'.

In the early 1770s John Gregory, an Edinburgh widower, was dying. As to how nigh his end was, he seems to have been remarkably unclear considering he was a doctor. Fretting about his two young daughters, he wrote, ostensibly for their benefit, a book of advice – not on their health, or how to save their souls (he was too urbane for that) – but on how to conduct themselves in polite society. In the eighteenth century, such 'advice books' played an important part in the education of every well-to-do girl. This book, *A*

Father's Legacy to his Daughters (1774), is undoubtedly a classic of its kind.

The general principle recommended by Gregory is that young women should live according to social expectations. They should appear innocent, ignorant, and 'delicate'. Social conventions are seldom questioned by Gregory. It is enough that young women should understand these conventions and follow them. In this way they will earn respect, and make themselves agreeable to men. Young women need to be well thought of by men, says Gregory, because their best chance of happiness lies in a successful marriage.

While today, following Rousseau, we may criticize some established patterns of behaviour as merely conventional, Gregory chooses not to exploit any distinction between the conventional and the natural. Gregory's advice is justified ultimately, like so much in the eighteenth century, as an extension of Nature's intentions for his daughters: 'I do not want to *make* you anything. I want to know what Nature has made you, and to perfect you on her plan' (Gregory, 1774, p. 62).

So courtship among young humans is effectively interpreted along the same lines as courtship among birds – it is all part of the same grand design in which some are pursued while others are pursuers. For a woman, according to Gregory, the fact that she is pursued may itself make the pursuer attractive; hence it is not absolutely necessary that the man should be attractive in the first place, 'As ... Nature has not given you that unlimited range in your choice which we enjoy she has wisely and benevolently assigned to you a greater flexibility of taste on this subject' (p. 91).

Challenges to such ideas often went unrecognized or unheard, since women were not expected to express opinions on such matters, nor, it was supposed, would they wish to. Gregory advises his daughters to be:

> ... rather silent in company, especially in a large one. People of sense and discernment will never mistake such silence for dullness. One may take a share in conversation without uttering a

syllable. The expression in the countenance shows it, and this never escapes an observing eye. (p. 33)

Like many male writers of the time, Gregory is here describing a desired model, rather than prevailing practice: he is hoping to check deviations from the ideal and ensure that women remain in their place. Typically, he laments the 'present mode of female manners', in which women are to be seen 'conversing with us with the same unreserved freedom as we do with one another'. This development Gregory attributes to women's desire to achieve power over men. But the strategy is declared to be self-defeating, on the grounds that the adoption of male forms of behaviour is both unattractive and unnatural in women.

Gregory himself points out that men prefer women who have a religion, since religious women are more likely to make better and faithful wives. So it is no surprise to find him advising girls to avoid 'sceptical treatises'. Religion also acts as a necessary check on women's 'natural vivacity'. Of course, vivacity has never been more of a female characteristic than a male one, but the real difference is that, in women, vivacity can be a problem. 'Wit', says Gregory, 'is the most dangerous talent you can possess' (p. 35). Dangerous to men, no doubt, and with true insight Gregory points out: 'If you appear to be men's equal, you will be thought to be assuming superiority' (p. 36).

If women wish to avoid arousing male hostility, they have to play a part – of innocence and ignorance. Once this is accepted, of course, there seems to be clear, negative implications for education. There is, however, according to Gregory, nothing wrong with girls reading (provided this is not carried to such lengths as to damage their health) or even with learning.

But if you happen to have any learning, keep it a profound secret, especially from the men, who generally look with a jealous and malignant eye on a woman of great parts and a cultivated understanding. (pp. 36–7)

13

Gregory's lack of enthusiasm for education for girls is thus not due to any view of their inability to profit from it. He sees nothing odd in the idea that women are as clever as men. But the appearance of ignorance is desirable even among intelligent women, and the appearance of sexual ignorance is especially desirable: 'no man of spirit and delicacy ever valued a heart much hackneyed in the ways of love' (p. 78).

So, on this view, women have to play a subordinate role to men, and one that will be pleasing, but not threatening. If they are clever, they should pretend not to be. If they are educated, they should pretend ignorance. Here we see the kind of way in which male perceptions of a woman's role in eighteenth-century society are interrelated with what is deemed to be an appropriate education for young ladies. It is possible, then, for well-to-do girls to be educated: some girls are clever, and (as Gregory points out) they were destined to spend many hours in solitude. But (at least in the eyes of many men) it was not necessary for them to be educated, and while seeing nothing improper in young women reading for diversion, Gregory advises that women would do better to cultivate sewing and knitting in order to fill the empty hours.

Another best–seller in its day was *Sermons to Young Women* (1765) by a fashionable London preacher, the Reverend James Fordyce. Mary Wollstonecraft writes that the *Sermons* had:

> ... long made a part of a young woman's library; nay, girls at school are allowed to read them; but I should instantly dismiss them from my pupil's if I wished to strengthen her understanding ...
>
> (Wollstonecraft, 1792, p. 191)

The unstated guiding principle which underlies Fordyce's writing is that women will want to be whatever men wish them to be. While Fordyce's views are supported by references to divine intentions, because of his sex he is able to tell women what is required if they wish to please men. His advice, if followed, he argues, would therefore be beneficial to both sexes. Like many eighteenth-century moralists, Fordyce stresses the pleasures of giving: but here his argument is blatantly self-interested, since his concern is with the pleasure women can derive from being good to men!

How then should women conduct themselves? We can pick out two points which Fordyce stresses, and note the kind of argument which he advances in support of his views. First, even though women appear to be endowed with more feeble minds to match their more feeble bodies, women should be encouraged to read. This is a much more positive statement than Gregory's view which is that there could be no objection to women reading, but that they might be better advised to spend their time on other and more appropriate pursuits. Fordyce's reasons for thinking women should read, however, are not primarily educational. Reading, he argues, is a convenient form of high-quality entertainment which can continue to give women pleasure, even when their beauty goes into decline and they cease to have the satisfaction of the attentions of men. But reading is also a safe pleasure. Impetuous females, 'their passions naturally ardent', are seen as easily attracted by ready pleasures without considering the dangers and drawbacks: reading, it is to be hoped, may make women more reflective.

One reason, Fordyce supposes, why women do not study as much as they might is their fear of appearing learned. They should, however, rest assured. Only a few of them, he observes, are likely to reach this stage. And in any case, male objections are not to real learning, but to the displays put on by women who have only a little learning. Nothing is said about men who pretend to more knowledge than they have. Fordyce may not recognize this as a possibility; but more likely this is not seen as a problem. What is a problem is that women are often boring: 'Consider the emptiness, insipidity, and inelegance of their conversation – how contemptible!' (Fordyce, 1765, vol. 2, p. 17). Cultivating a taste for reading would prevent women from sinking to these low levels of esteem by raising their minds beyond the common female

15

preoccupation with dress and appearance. This is not to say that women are to blame for this pursuit of good looks. Ultimately the fault lies with men because they praise beauty so much. And Fordyce also invokes divine authority for telling women that they have a duty to make themselves attractive, since it is this which 'can lead to a state for which they were manifestly formed'.

The second theme to be noted from *Sermons to Young Women* is again given theological backing. 'The Almighty has thrown you upon the protection of our sex' (vol. 1, p. 9). Because of this, women have a duty to require protection! A whole sermon is devoted to 'meekness'. Men expect timidity in women. Fordyce tells his audience: 'fearfulness to a certain degree becomes you'. Any who fail to exhibit the appropriate characteristics will suffer what Fordyce again assumes to be a serious penalty: they will be deprived of male attention.

> ... a worthy woman, shrinking from manifest hazard, or threatened violence, we are always forward and proud to protect; while, on the other hand, an intrepid female seems to renounce our aid, and in some respect to invade our province. We turn away and leave her to herself. (vol. 2, p. 224)

What is interesting here is that while reading and learning in women are seen as acceptable, physical prowess is seen as a serious threat to the natural order. There is nothing necessarily wrong, according to Fordyce, with a woman being cleverer than a man (provided this is not too obvious), but a woman who is physically superior 'would surely to a civilised nature suggest shocking ideas'. As a preacher, Fordyce has a different model for his female readers:

> Your best emblem, beloved, is the smiling form of Peace, robed in white, and bearing a branch of olive. Like the apostles and first Christians, your highest glory is to conquer by benignity and triumph by patience. (vol. 2, p. 223)

It may seem surprising that this should be considered particularly desirable for women, rather than for people of either sex. The explanation seems to be that instead of thinking in terms of virtue *per se*, Fordyce thinks in terms of female virtues and male virtues, a view which was challenged by Mary Wollstonecraft.

Fordyce always gauges the merits of women's behaviour simply on its tendency to promote harmonious relationships with men. Hence the emphasis on soft compliance and meek submission – characteristics whose absence in females would, in his view, impair such relationships and lead to the unhappiness of both parties. And, warns Fordyce, it is pointless for women to complain after they have alienated their husbands:

> ... had you behaved to them with a more respectful observance ... studying their humour, overlooking their mistakes, complaining as seldom as possible, and making it your daily care to relieve their anxieties ... your house might at this day have been the abode of domestic bliss.   (vol. 2, p. 265)

Sermons is, therefore, a further instance of a treatise on human behaviour which is sanctioned by appeals to male authority. Even here, what are supposedly revelations about God's intentions for the women he designed and created really amount to nothing more than statements about what men expect of women. Yet even this is not quite strong enough: the *Sermons* explain not just what kind of behaviour men *desired*, but what men *required* of women. Nevertheless, if some of Fordyce's theological arguments appear highly dubious and self-interested, it is important to remember that the scriptures are clear on the position of women, at least as interpreted by the translators of King James's Bible:

> Unto the woman he said, I will greatly multiply thy sorrow and thy conception; in sorrow thou shalt bring forth children; and thy desire shall be to thy husband, and he shall rule over thee.
> (Genesis 3: 16)

If much of what Gregory and Fordyce have to say reads like a loosely constructed miscellany of fairly superficial thoughts, which nevertheless reflect the views of many men at the time, we might reasonably hope for better when we turn to our third conservative writer, Jean-Jacques Rousseau. Using the term 'conservative' in connection with Rousseau may seem surprising. After all, his political philosophy is often credited with having lit the long, slow fuse that led to the French Revolution. Seeing the differences of social rank as superficial and irrelevant, Rousseau in *Emile* and elsewhere stresses the basic sameness of all men. He is, however, much more impressed by the differences between male and female: so his egalitarianism does not extend to anything that we would recognize as equality between the sexes. While Rousseau's general educational theory seems progressive and enlightened, this is intended to inform the education of boys only. There is not much to admire in what he proposes for the education of girls.

Among the principles governing the curriculum of his fictitious male pupil are three which have been especially admired. First, Emile should have unlimited scope for play: this is advocated partly on humanitarian grounds, and partly because of the learning potential inherent in such activity. Second, Emile is not to be pressurized into studying: learning will be acquired when the child develops the appropriate interests and capacities. Third, Emile is not to be directly taught: instead he should be encouraged to think things out for himself and to draw conclusions from his own experience.

As well as giving this well-known account of the education of Emile, Rousseau's treatise also describes the 'ideal' curriculum for a girl. (This programme is proposed for another fictitious character called Sophie.) In Rousseau's account of Sophie's education all the principles outlined above are reversed. Sophie is to have little freedom. Her play, says Rousseau, ought to be frequently interrupted so that she learns to put up with life's irritations. Instead of learning being pursued in accordance with the learner's own pace and inclinations, Sophie's lack of application in arithmetic lessons is to be combated by rewarding good work with cherries. Instead of exercising her own judgement of religious questions, she is to be taught religious doctrines, without going into the reasons for holding them.

Rousseau's underlying justification for this difference in strategy is that girls' education cannot be the same as boys' education, because girls are not the same as boys. Rousseau sees the female as more modest, more cunning, more understanding of the opposite sex and more skilled in personal relationships. The things women lack are concentration, accuracy, moderation in both religious faith and sexual desire, skill in abstract disciplines and good judgement in literary matters. Rousseau's explanation of these differences between the sexes is that they are complementary and that male and female are intended to pool their native resources: 'Woman has more wit, man more genius; woman observes, man reasons; together they provide the clearest light and the profoundest knowledge which is possible to the unaided mind' (Rousseau, 1762, p. 350). But this division of talents hardly suggests a partnership between equals, and Rousseau maintains that the law of nature bids the woman obey the man. It is also significant that Emile's development is explained in its own terms, while Sophie's nature is explained in terms of how it differs from Emile's.

Perhaps the most important difference in his curricular proposals for girls and boys is that while Rousseau explicitly rules out the preparation of boys for any specific future role, a girl's education is to be conducted in the light of the destiny which her nature determines. Men, he says, are only sometimes men, but women are always women. Females should play the role of obedient wife, mother and homemaker, and girls should be educated with this future in mind.

Why does Rousseau believe in the importance and rightness of the woman's role, as he perceives it? In the first place he suggests that it has always been like this. The traditional role he prescribes for women is more generally accepted the further back you go in history; and, for Rousseau, earlier times are closer to a true state of nature, and therefore morally superior. Further, the nature of the sex act shows that the male is intended to dominate and the female is meant to please. Physiologically, the female is made for child-care; her domestic role is essential for the prospering of family life; and any subsequent change of role is supposedly injurious to her health. Finally, a woman will not flourish in male occupations ('a woman is worth less as a man'); she should follow the role for which she was intended, rather than rebel against nature.

These intentions are manifest at an early age; every young girl likes sewing, says Rousseau, and loves playing with dolls. This, he concludes, 'shows her instinctive bent towards her life's work'. It is notable that while in other contexts Rousseau is very much alive to the power of environmental influence, and the likelihood of children acquiring ideas which are prevalent in society, his explanation of girls' interests are nevertheless given in terms of instinct and a 'grand design'.

The design of nature, according to Rousseau, means that the future role of every girl is laid down in advance. This role determines what every female needs – essentially, male admiration and respect. This need in turn dictates the curriculum for girls. 'They should learn many things, but only such things as are appropriate' (Rousseau, 1762, p. 327). These include learning to be pleasing, learning to submit to male authority, and acquiring useful accomplishments. One such accomplishment is the art of conversing agreeably with their husbands: for this, girls require an education that transcends the more menial domestic arts. They may, for example, be introduced to logic and metaphysics but they 'should only skim the surface'. A girl's curriculum must from start to finish be designed for the benefit of men; but since women are dependent on men's goodwill, this kind of instruction will also be to the benefit of the female pupil.

Rousseau's views on the nature of girls' education are therefore directly related to his views on the proper place of women: indeed he treats the two questions as a single issue. Here, his thinking is conservative, even by the standards of his time. He presents his position as a call to return to the ways of nature, and he criticizes the contemporary loss of respect for the traditional sexual division of labour. He complains that men are working in shops and in the tailoring trade while women set themselves up as literary critics.

Wollstonecraft responded to these views with flair, passion, and cool analysis. The end of the eighteenth century was a time of political, social, and intellectual turmoil. The French Revolution had injected into the public mind a sense of the power of ideas, and social change appeared imminent. Arguments about social justice were committed to paper in haste, often in the form of pamphlets. Mary Wollstonecraft wrote an entire book in six weeks, with the printer working on one chapter while the next was being written. The logical sequel to an earlier work which she had written in defence of the principles of the French Revolution, *Vindication of the Rights of Woman* was a manifesto for a different kind of social upheaval: justice for women.

Dedicating the book to Talleyrand, a French bishop who had decided that his allegiance lay with the Revolution rather than with Rome, Wollstonecraft wrote:

> If the abstract rights of man will bear discussion and explanation, those of women, by a parity of reasoning, will not shrink from the same test ... Consider ... whether, when men contend for their freedom, and to be allowed to judge for themselves respecting their own happiness, it be not inconsistent and unjust to subjugate women, even though you firmly believe that you are acting in the manner best calculated to promote their happiness? Who made man the exclusive judge, if woman partake with him of the gift of reason?
>
> (Wollstonecraft, 1792, p. 87)

Despite the gift of reason, however, Wollstonecraft felt that women's behaviour was often frivolous, manipulative, and guided by ignorance. But unlike the male authors she criticized with a mixture of insight and derision, she did not consider this to be a natural or inevitable state; women learned to be like this. Playing a subordinate role in a male-dominated society, they were denied access to education and political rights, and therefore mastered the strategies necessary for those in such subordinate positions:

> Asserting the rights which women in common with men ought to contend for, I have not attempted to extenuate their faults; but to prove them to be the natural consequence of their education and station in society. (p. 319)

Women's behaviour, according to Wollstonecraft, was to be explained in terms of their circumstances. 'From the tyranny of man, I firmly believe, the greater number of female follies proceed' (p. 318).

The implication is that if the circumstances could be radically altered, this would enable women's reason to develop, and their behaviour to change. Reason was the foundation of virtue, and since women and men were equipped with the same rationality, what was virtue for one was virtue for the other. Wollstonecraft therefore rejected the meek qualities praised by Fordyce, not because gentleness had no place, but because it had been claimed to be peculiarly fitting for women.

> ... if fear in girls, instead of being cherished, perhaps *created*, were treated in the same manner as cowardice in boys, we should quickly see women with more dignified aspects. It is true, they could not then with equal propriety be termed the sweet flowers that smile in the walk of man; but they would be more respectable members of society, and discharge the important duties of life by the light of their own reason. 'Educate women like men,' says Rousseau, 'and the more they resemble our sex the less power they will have over us.' This is the very point I aim at. I do not wish them to have power over men; but over themselves.
> (p. 154, italics added)

Wollstonecraft therefore argued for the empowerment of women. She maintained that women should be viewed as rational human beings, with equal worth, and not in negative terms by reference to the expectations and requirements of men. This meant that women should be allowed to develop their rationality without hindrance. In practical terms, Wollstonecraft (remarkably) advocated a national system of co-educational schooling, where provision of the same curriculum for both sexes would give girls valuable experience of the 'jostlings of equality'.

Wollstonecraft maintained that educating everyone together would foster genuine understanding between the sexes and lead to more fulfilling relationships within marriage. With the gaining of self-respect, women could no longer be expected to show obsequiousness or blind obedience. For a devotee of reason, such behaviour could not be seen as virtuous anyway: but clearly the change was potentially threatening to men. Yet – unlike Gregory, Fordyce, and Rousseau – Wollstonecraft believed that equitable relations between the sexes would benefit men as well as women.

> Would men but generously snap our chains, and be content with rational fellowship instead of slavish obedience, they would find us more observant daughters, more affectionate sisters, more faithful wives, more reasonable mothers – in a word better citizens. We should then love them with true affection, because we should learn to respect ourselves. (p. 263)

It would be misleading to suggest that such liberal views were wholly the preserve of women. As a newly elected Member of Parliament, John Stuart Mill introduced the first bill proposing votes for women some seventy years after the death of Mary Wollstonecraft. And nearly eighty years after the publication of *A Vindication of the Rights of Woman,* Mill thought it 'presumption' for anyone to 'pretend to decide what women are or are not, can or cannot be, by natural constitution' (Mill, 1869, pp. 304–5). He considered women's character to be 'an eminently artificial thing – the result of forced repression in some directions, unnatural stimulation in others' (p. 276).

23

Mill saw that one had to go beyond appearances. Anticipating the development of twentieth-century psychology, he could see that in due course it might be possible to explain differences in behaviour between the sexes in terms of the different influences to which each sex was exposed. Also, there were obvious ways of accounting for women's relative lack of achievement which were more persuasive than accounts which depended on inherent incapacity. Women, he thought, had never been given the necessary educational opportunities.

Mill advanced four different kinds of objection to the subordination of women to men, and to the effective exclusion of all women from a large range of occupations. First, many of these jobs bring status and fulfilment: the exclusion of women therefore means that they are deprived. The rearing of children is certainly an important job, but it lasts for only a limited period of time. Secondly, having all spheres of life open to women would (potentially) harness double the amount of talent available for serving society. Thirdly, and importantly, the existing arrangement also has an undesirable effect on the development of boys. Simply by living in this kind of society, boys learn that they are, by virtue of their sex, superior to half the human race, regardless of any talents or abilities they may (or may not) possess. In effect boys are taught that they have the right to rule by virtue of belonging to the dominant group – a principle which Mill wished to see rooted out in society generally.

This brings us to Mill's fourth, and most pervasive, consideration: the continued legal subordination of women was an indefensible injustice. Armed with a reformer's sense of social progress, Mill saw that women's position had become increasingly anomalous. The tyranny of slavery had been abolished, and the British had got rid of absolute monarchy. These were important developments because, in Mill's view, to be subjected to undue power was 'naturally and necessarily humiliating'.

The arguments of Wollstonecraft and Mill, amongst others,

were influential, but in practice many of the basic rights necessary for a just society continued to be denied to women. The establishment view towards the end of the nineteenth century was clearly stated by a woman at the very top of the social order, Queen Victoria:

> The Queen is most anxious to enlist everyone who can speak or write to join in checking this mad, wicked folly of 'Woman's Rights' with all its attendant horrors, on which her poor feeble sex is bent, forgetting every sense of womanly feeling and propriety ... It is a subject which makes the Queen so furious that she cannot contain herself. God created men and women different – then let them remain each in their own position.
>
> (quoted in Friedan, 1965, p. 114)

In a male-dominated society, traditional views of a woman's place were too firmly entrenched for there to be equal educational provision for the female half of the population. The medical establishment, for example, was of the opinion that excessive study was injurious to women's health: it was not in their nature to be able to cope with undue mental effort. In 1886 the President of the British Medical Association cautioned:

> From the eagerness of woman's nature competitive brainwork among gifted girls can hardly but be excessive, especially if the competition be against the superior brain-weight and brain-strength of man. The resulting ruin can be averted – if it be averted at all – only by drawing so largely upon the woman's whole capital stock of vital force and energy as to leave a remainder quite inadequate for maternity. (quoted in Purvis, 1991, p. 3)

Despite the existence of such highly conservative views, there was increased access to some areas of employment for women. In particular, very large numbers came into the teaching profession in the period after 1870, to the extent that by the turn of the century, although predominantly in subordinate positions, women formed the mainstay of the profession.

25

(A historical perspective on the position of women in school-teaching from 1870 onwards will be the subject of Chapter 3.) Incongruously, however, women's suffrage had to wait for realization until 1918, when it was achieved through women's own efforts and actions. And it was not until the 1970s that society felt compelled to begin seriously to rethink women's traditional role.

2 Before the Sex Discrimination Act

1970 has been called a 'bonanza year' for feminism (Spender, 1985, p. 26), the turning point when feminist analysis acquired a mature radicalism, and began to capture more widespread interest and support. This year saw the publication of, amongst others, Germaine Greer's *The Female Eunuch*, Kate Millett's *Sexual Politics*, and Shulamith Firestone's *The Dialectic of Sex*. It is also generally recognized that the preceding decade was one of considerable social change, and in this chapter we will focus on this period which set the social context within which the new feminism was launched. During the 1960s, ideas of equality and liberty gained ground, and came to command widespread, if moderate, support. The general acceptance of such ideas within the mainstream of society provided an important foothold from which the programme of the women's movement was later able to effect some advance. What is curious, however, is that in the potentially sympathetic climate of that decade there was often a general blindness among those in positions of power to the particular problems of the female situation. Indeed it will be argued at the end of this chapter that in education some apparently enlightened thinking was inimical to advancing the schooling of girls.

If some people felt more free in the 1960s than before, what did they see themselves as being liberated from? The whole decade has been seen as a rejection of the 'old ways'. This is perhaps best symbolized in the idea of a 'generation gap' between old and young people. J. F. Kennedy came in, and the patrician Harold Macmillan went out. His successor as Prime

Minister, Sir Alec Douglas-Home (described by Macmillan as 'the old governing class at its best') seemed to represent all that was unacceptable to the new prejudices of the British public. He was therefore ill-placed to fight off a Labour leader who deliberately presented himself as someone whose ideas were more relevant to the demands of the modern world, a world of new technologies and new opportunities.

Conventions and authority were challenged, and there was a strong reaction among the disaffected young against what were seen as the out-moded and discredited values of the older generation. A common charge levelled at the establishment generally was one of hypocrisy. Hence the significance of the title of the Bishop of Woolwich's *succès de scandale*, *Honest to God* (Robinson, 1963), a theological work which seemed to leave atheists and sceptics with little to dispute.

Liberation from the conventions and hypocrisy of the past was seen to take many forms, including the supposed sexual liberation of women which was associated with the increased availability of the contraceptive pill. The Pope deliberated at great length on the ethics of contraception, causing one lyricist to write 'I hope the Pope makes up his mind before my man gets in'; and his eventual reaffirmation of traditional Catholic teaching provoked an unprecedented challenge to his own authority. Many British Catholics decided to ignore or disobey the encyclical, and were often supported by their own priests. The Bishop of Woolwich wrote: 'Few will now bother to ask whether the Pope is infallible: they are more concerned with whether the pill is infallible' (quoted in Levin, 1970, p. 116).

The benefits to women of the new sexual mores have been much debated. Some have seen the widespread acceptance of contraception as giving women a new control over their bodies (perhaps at a cost to their bodies) while others have portrayed the 'permissive society' in general as yet another instance of the exploitation of women. For some women expectations were raised: educated women *felt* equal, but in practical terms they still found themselves occupying a secondary role. There was much talk of the right of the individual to be different at this time, but in reality there were strong pressures, especially on the young, to conform to the reaction against the repressive conventions of the establishment – a reaction which often had a distinctively male voice. Nevertheless, puritanism had gone, and by the end of the decade, so had the Lord Chamberlain, whose function had been to censor plays.

Education was clearly not going to remain insulated from such wide-ranging social changes and ways of thinking. A less formal set of relationships between teacher and taught was to varying degrees established in all types of educational institution, from the university to the primary school. And the general social reaction against the 'old ways' also produced a radical shift in educational thought and practice, most notably in the primary school. The move towards a more indulgent treatment of children, coupled with a demand for respect for the individual, resulted in the liberal progressivism of the Plowden Report (1967) and, in Scotland, the Primary Memorandum (SED, 1965). These official reports drew heavily on a philosophy which had long been familiar to theorists, but which had, in practical terms, been marginalized. Originating from Rousseau, this philosophy was informed by a radical view of knowledge and learning.

What passes for knowledge in schools, it was argued, is often not really knowledge at all: it makes no real impact, is not permanent, and involves no real understanding. Real knowledge (as distinct from the superficial learning required for public examinations) is only achieved when people want to learn or need to learn. What people need to learn depends on their ways of making sense of their experience and on the nature of that experience; and this varies according to the individual. Therefore learning cannot be provided for through a fixed curriculum of subject matter defined by others as valuable. Nor can we plan on the basis of what a pupil will need to know to function adequately in tomorrow's world – society changes too quickly and in ways that are unpredictable. The

29

best strategy for genuine educational development would therefore be to make available to the pupil a range of possible learning experiences which can be chosen according to the interests of the individual.

This approach, which involves greater respect for the pupil-as-learner and suggests that the curriculum should be, if not determined by, then at least sensitive to the needs and interests of individual pupils, acquired widespread acceptance among primary teachers from the 1960s onwards. The Plowden Report and the Primary Memorandum effectively promoted this approach in a way which would have been inconceivable thirty years earlier. One reason, perhaps, being that these official reports assumed that a curriculum which was sensitive to the needs and interests of the individual would also, inevitably, be one which provided children with a preparation for the wider economic and social demands of the modern world. Equally significant was the success of A. S. Neill's *Summerhill*, published in 1968, in which Neill expounded a much more radical version of liberal progressivism.

The new respect for individuals contained an egalitarian element – or perhaps two egalitarian elements. The first was a notion of equal worth – a protest against the process of labelling some individuals as unsuccessful, and so of less value, whether within education or in society at large. The less 'able' members of any society, it was now emphasized, have an equal entitlement to dignity and self-respect. The second (and related) notion was one of equality of access. Barriers to status and socio-economic resources were to be broken down, particularly through the process of schooling. A just education system should not serve simply to legitimize an individual's position in society, but should instead provide individuals with the environment and opportunities necessary to the development of their true potential. Together, these two ideas proved highly influential in the formation of educational policy.

In some areas, the principle of equality was seen to make a real impact on the system. One egalitarian reform from the

1960s into the 1970s was the development of comprehensive schooling, which involved abandoning the process of 'selection' for a grammar school education by examination at the end of primary school. Selection processes had seemed unreliable. It was felt that youngsters from less-advantaged homes inevitably showed up less well than their middle-class counterparts: giving them a 'lesser' education merely compounded the problem and made it difficult for them to prove themselves at a later stage. There was a clear need to prevent what was seen as 'wasted' ability within the system. However, it was further argued that if one aimed actually to compensate for disadvantage, one would have to look beyond secondary schooling to the earlier stages of education. This gave rise to the Plowden Report's concept of 'educational priority areas', and the proposal to identify underprivileged localities whose primary schools would receive additional educational resources. At the time, this was seen as tackling inequality at its roots.

From the new discipline of the sociology of education, the influence of A. H. Halsey and colleagues also began to be felt at the beginning of the 1960s (Floud *et al.*, 1956; Halsey *et al.*, 1961). From the perspectives of both theoretician and policy-maker, however, inequalities were thought of predominantly in terms either of scholastic ability or social class, or the relationship between the two. What seems surprising with hindsight is the lack of an explicit and clearly articulated gender perspective within this. It was not that the potential importance of gender as a social factor went wholly unnoticed at the time, but it was apparently not high on the agenda of most researchers, educationalists or policy-makers. Thus, the period throughout the 1960s saw a growing concern with ideas of equality in education, but the principal focus of these concerns was on educational disadvantage as characterized by social class position.

Not everyone was sympathetic to such egalitarian ideals or to the new progressivism in education. Opposition to liberal change was spearheaded in the 1960s and the 1970s by a series of Black Papers whose main concern was to re-establish traditional patterns of authority and order, and to block the currents which seemed to threaten these. While the editors and writers themselves frequently occupied positions of authority – headteachers and professors – they claimed, not implausibly, to represent an unheard body of public opinion. In the first Black Paper, published in 1969, John Sparrow, Warden of All Souls, Oxford, wrote dismissively about 'egalitarian idealists', claiming that 'they realize the truth of the idea against which they are protesting – the idea that some people are indeed, through no fault of their own, inferior to other people' (Cox and Dyson, 1969, p. 65). Whether this includes women as a social group or not – 'through no fault of their own' – is not clear, although one might expect that part of the return to such values would include the reaffirmation of woman's traditional role in society.

So what of women's own situation at this time, as perceived by women? We have to go back some years to the beginning of the decade, and to the ground-breaking work of Betty Friedan. In 1963 Friedan published a treatise based on conversations with well-off white American women. What these women actually experienced in their lives was a total mismatch between the rhetoric of womanhood and the reality. Women were supposed to be content in their traditional role. Those who expressed dissatisfaction earned a hostile response: either they did not realize how lucky they were to be provided for without having to go out to work, or else they were defective as women. Friedan judged women to be trapped in this dilemma without being able to articulate the problem. Describing it as 'the problem that has no name' she remedied this with the phrase 'the feminine mystique', which was also the title of her book.

The solution to the problem, in Friedan's eyes, was to create a more satisfactory image for women. Women themselves would bring this about by going out to work, or more precisely, by pursuing careers, since Friedan's reference points were all middle-class women. However, the representations made by Friedan and others in the NOW (National Organization of Women) group to the Equal Employment Opportunity Commission went unheard, and their proposals were not even included on the agenda. (The Commission was originally set up in the early years of the Kennedy administration to investigate women's status.) The idea that men dominate and control our culture had resurfaced, and more radical answers to the 'problem that has no name' were formulated.

Perhaps the best known of the feminist books published in 1970 is Germaine Greer's *The Female Eunuch*. Her most notorious line is 'Women have very little idea how much men hate them'. Hatred, according to Greer, is manifested in pornography and violence and in the many demeaning words for women in common usage. Greer's strategy is to hit back. While Wollstonecraft had argued that men would actually find liberated women more agreeable, Greer suggests the opposite. The road to liberation involves making trouble, being threatening, and acting defiantly, since engaging in this kind of activity establishes for women that they are free, powerful people. In particular, showing male claims to superiority to be absurd is a challenge women must learn to make. And a crucial liberating move is for a woman to free herself from any desire to fulfil male expectations, certainly contradicting the traditional view, as expressed by Rousseau, that fundamentally women were made to please men.

The idea of self-discovery through defiant action is persuasive. But was this kind of empowerment for women actually going to reduce male power? Power based on claims that can be shown to be ridiculous may well be undermined, and yet, would this alone really undermine the social structures and institutions which maintained women in a subordinate position? Power is the key concept in Kate Millett's account of the struggle for women's rights. Power is held by men, often in more subtle forms, like the power to define situations and identify what is to count as a problem. Rule by men Millett calls 'patriarchy'. Men seek to hold on to power and privilege; therefore resistance implies struggle.

The work of Shulamith Firestone provides a further perspective on male domination. She points out that the history of women's struggle is relatively unknown. Her explanation for this is twofold. Many women may be uninterested in militant feminism, seeing it as having little relevance now that women appear to be emancipated into male society: for example, they have the vote and access to universities. More subtly, however, history is written by men. Men decide what is significant and what should be drawn to people's attention: hence the non-appearance of the story of the struggle for women's rights.

From these feminist perspectives, a key question is: what is the relationship between education and the position of women? Firestone has the most radical message, arguing that children are as oppressed as women, and both are abused by men:

> We must include the oppression of children in any programme for feminist revolution or we will be subject to the same failing of which we have so often accused men; of not having gone deep enough in our analysis, of having missed an important substratum of oppression merely because it didn't directly concern *us* ... we have developed, in our long period of related sufferings, a certain compassion and understanding for them that there is no reason to lose now; we know where they're at, what they're experiencing, because we, too, are still undergoing the same kind of oppressions.
>
> (Firestone, 1972, pp. 101–2)

Firestone draws on the 'invention of childhood' theory which portrays the evolution of this concept, with its connotations of innocence, helplessness and immaturity, as a conspiracy against children. These alleged characteristics of childhood are used to legitimate their subordination, in which process schooling is seen to play a leading part.

For some radicals, the liberation of children – female and male – required the abolition of school. Schools were institutions which confirmed and justified male dominance through the lessons of the past. They were also institutions which socialized children to expect and accept male power. Kate Millett, for example, saw education as an instrument of patriarchy

> ... assigning the humanities and certain social sciences (at least in their lower or marginal branches) to the female – and science and technology, the professions, business and engineering to the male. Of course the balance of employment, prestige and reward at present lie with the latter. ... The humanities, because not exclusively male, suffer in prestige: the sciences, technology, and business, because they are nearly exclusively male reflect the deformation of the 'masculine' personality, eg, a certain predatory or aggressive character. (Millett, 1971, p. 42)

The extent to which such cultural divisions are still reflected in the subjects taken by male and female pupils in schools at the present time will be explored later in the book using empirical evidence. Millett's point is important, but there are a number of perspectives on this. Science and technology may well occupy positions of high status in our society, and they may also clearly represent elements of patriarchy. But is the response to challenge the status of these disciplines in schools, or is it a matter of ensuring and promoting access to such subjects for girls? Similarly, what of the status of stereotypically 'female' subjects?

Germaine Greer takes a much more positive view of some aspects of girls' educational experiences, seeing school as a potential antidote to home-life and to mothers. Girls are forcibly 'feminized' by their mothers, and excessively protected, 'taught to fear and distrust the world at large, for reasons which are never clearly stated ...' (Greer, 1970, p. 86). Others, as we have seen above, are not so convinced. Do schools create, reinforce or challenge stereotyped gender roles – for both girls and boys?

Betty Friedan is perhaps most positive about the value of education. Her belief was that 'for women, as well as men, education is and must be the matrix of human evolution' (Friedan, 1965, p. 322). We can recognize in this the increasing presence over the last few decades of the mature female student in higher education. And this is a phenomenon which Friedan saw as having great significance.

> ... more and more women, with virtually no help from society and with belated and begrudging encouragement from educators themselves, are going back to school to get the education they need. Their determination betrays women's underestimated human strength and their urgent need to use it.
>
> (Friedan, 1965, p. 317)

So far we have argued that the 1960s saw the emergence of a general adherence to principles of equality and liberty which greatly influenced the development of educational policy. These educational developments, however, were pursued with little true recognition, at least by those in positions to influence policy, either of women's disadvantaged position within society or of the possible contribution that education might make to altering, as opposed to maintaining, this situation. We now argue that the problem goes deeper than this: it is not just that ideas were never connected, but that there is a degree of tension between attempts to address gender inequalities and some seemingly enlightened educational ideas which were beginning to be implemented at this time.

Specifically, in curriculum terms, there is a potential problem in the pervasive influence from the 1960s onwards of a liberal, progressive philosophy. Educationalists of this period were surely correct in seeing that the education of the early years was the most crucial part of the process, but at the very least, as far as the development of girls is concerned, there are clear dangers and limitations in Plowden-style progressivism. To elucidate the tension between progressivism and feminist concerns, the theory underlying this approach to education will now be examined in more detail.

The essence of the progressive critique of traditional schooling is that its conception of learning is 'ill-matched to' or 'not in harmony with' the nature of those whom it purports to educate. So progressive writers from Rousseau onwards have spent much time and space explaining to readers what children are really like, how they develop, and how the curriculum should reflect their needs and interests.

The Plowden Report declares:

> At the heart of the educational process lies the child. No advances in policy ... have their desired effect unless they are in harmony with the nature of the child, unless they are fundamentally acceptable to him [*sic*]. (Plowden Committee, 1967, p. 7)

But what is the nature of a child, or indeed the nature of a human being? And how is it to be known? Rousseau's *Emile* is useful here as it serves to highlight the difficulty of characterizing this kind of foundation objectively. What is transparent in *Emile* is the extent to which Rousseau's account of woman's needs and nature was determined by his view of the ideal society. Rousseau claimed that women were designed by nature for a specific and subordinate role, and that this traditional social/sexual arrangement ensured compatibility between the sexes. Where the social premise is suppressed, however, it may prove even harder to challenge what is presented as 'fact': and this was manifestly a difficulty for earlier feminist thinkers. For example, what 'evidence' was there to challenge the orthodoxy of religious teachings, if the subordinate position of women was neither natural nor preordained?

In 1944 the Norwood Report claimed that there were three kinds of pupil, each needing a different kind of education. Some children were said to be 'interested in learning for its own sake' and 'able to grasp an argument'. There were others whose 'interests and abilities lie markedly in the field of applied science or applied art' for whom 'subtleties of language are too delicate'. And there was a third type whose mind 'must turn its knowledge or its curiosity to immediate (practical) test' (quoted in Lawton, 1977, Ch. 3). One cannot resist the conclusion that such perceptions are determined by the desirability of having children enter a stratified adult society at one of three levels. Wherever a subordinate role is envisaged, a limited and limiting curriculum is deemed appropriate. It is clear that, at least in the past, girls have been disadvantaged by just such an argument. So the concept of 'education according to nature' can be a reactionary dictum as well as a reforming one depending on the political perspectives of the user.

In the 1960s progressive theory tried to avoid the quicksands of subjectivism by basing itself on the rock of scientific research. The Primary Memorandum reflects this outlook:

> The pattern of education in the primary school years must ... above all have regard for the nature of the child and for the way he [*sic*] grows and develops during this period. In recent years research has yielded a considerable amount of information on these very points, and if education at the primary level is to meet the child's needs and interests, this body of knowledge must exercise a decisive influence on the attitude and practice of teachers.
>
> (SED, 1965, p. 3)

Two years later, the Plowden Report echoed the central idea:

> Knowledge of the manner in which children develop ... is of prime importance, both in avoiding educationally harmful practices and in introducing effective ones. In the last 50 years much work has been done on the physical, emotional and intellectual growth of children. There is a vast array of facts ...
>
> (Plowden Committee, 1967, p. 7)

In their enthusiastic embrace of developmental psychology, both documents fail to show any critical awareness of the possible limitations of this kind of empirical investigation. There seems to be an assumption that a progressive approach to education can be justified without introducing evaluative non-scientific considerations.

In so far as progressivism is built round the concept of the child's needs, however, this view is certainly open to question.

As R. F. Dearden points out, a need is not a characteristic that can be established by observation alone: to identify a child's needs one must go beyond Plowden's 'vast array of facts'. Someone's having a need involves an assumed purpose or desired end which can be achieved by fulfilling the 'need'. However, as Dearden puts it: 'One has to look behind statements of need to the values that are guiding them, for it is here that the issue substantially lies' (Dearden, 1968, p. 16).

Dearden's basic point holds good: what we judge children to need will depend on how we think they *ought* to develop. This question is not rigorously pursued by the Plowden Report which instead contents itself with the different question of how children actually *do* develop. Much development may be interest-led, and by contrast with 'needs', the notion of 'interests' is a relatively straightforward one. There is no logical difficulty in establishing empirically who has what interests when. Following Rousseau's report that girls like sewing and playing with dolls, it will now be useful to go on to examine some other observations made by progressives about the interests of girls.

The idea of an education which caters for each child's interests suggests designing a curriculum which allows choice between different activities according to the child's actual preferences. The school which developed this principle as far as it would go was A. S. Neill's Summerhill. Neill is generally seen as the most radical of progressive educationists, and he consistently argued that children should spend their time pursuing whatever interested them. Despite some critical remarks about our patriarchal society, Neill's brief discussions of the differences between male and female remain at an alarmingly superficial level. He notes, for example, that girls are more concerned with their appearance and are less active in school management; and that boys do more damage because, unlike girls, their fantasy life requires pirate ships and gangster hold-ups. Yet he offers no account of why the sexes differ in these ways. However, when he goes on to suggest that boys may be more creative than girls he becomes more reflective and conjectures that he may have acquired this impression because at Summerhill there is a lot of material which boys are interested in but girls are not – radios, engines, and a workshop with iron and wood (Neill, 1968, p. 29). But he does not then ask why these different patterns of interest have arisen: he merely accepts them. Such a casual noting of differences is hard to defend where every pupil's learning programme is directly determined by his or her actual interests.

The constraints of a more conventional classroom may impose limits on the scope for pursuing individual interests. Nevertheless, in its discussion of art and craft, the Primary Memorandum states: 'There is no reason other than that of expediency why all the members of the class should be occupied on similar tasks.' And it declares: 'Railway and aeroplane modelling has a strong appeal for many boys, as does doll's house furnishing for girls' (SED, 1965, p. 170). This line of thought is taken a step further when it is suggested that sewing techniques should be imparted to girls, but apparently not to boys. While the girls are learning sewing, the boys are no doubt learning sawing. This after all, seems to be the logic of an interest-based curriculum. The question is whether educators should accept such one-sided patterns of interest as 'natural', or view them as an undesirable kind of development which ought to be challenged.

It is clearly not enough to establish what children's interests are. We must also ask ourselves such questions as: What kind of interests would we like children to have? And how ought these interests to develop? From such evaluative questions there is no escape, whatever may be urged to the contrary by those progressives who adhere to Neill's non-interventionist principles. Surely it is a mistake to think that if the teacher deliberately refrains from implanting or cultivating interests in pupils, these pupils will grow up in a kind of vacuum which will permit self-determination? Even within specially designed environments like a Summerhill-style boarding school, wider society brings its own pressures to bear. These need to be evaluated so that it can be decided whether they should be welcomed, or resisted, or provided with a counterbalance. It is not enough to say, as the Primary Memorandum does, that: 'Education must ... have due regard ... for the attainments, qualities and attitudes which society will expect of him [sic] as an adult' (SED, 1965, p. 11). What if contemporary society puts a premium on people who are competitive, self-centred and uncaring? And what if society expects males to be dominant and females to be subordinate? Such questions are simply not considered.

Psychological descriptions based on observational studies of child development and, in particular, studies of the female's nature and of her needs and interests are likely to portray girls and women as society permits or requires them to be rather than as they could or should be. Even if it had been possible for psychological descriptions to be impartial – and perhaps not just another element of patriarchy – it is unlikely that this would have altered perspectives on gender inequalities at the time of the Primary Memorandum or the Plowden Report, assuming that such perspectives existed amongst educational policy-makers at all. The full educational development of girls required a distinctive vision of how things *ought* to be, a willingness to defend such value judgements, and a determination to intervene positively in the classroom to challenge some of the observed patterns of boys' and girls' development, and not just allow things to take their 'natural' course. Keeping girls occupied with doll's house furnishing does not look like a preparation for Plowden's vision of a society 'marked by rapid and far-reaching social change' (Plowden Committee, 1967, p. 186). Rather it is to reflect Rousseau's view that while the future for boys was quite uncertain, the future for girls was entirely predictable.

But if the emphasis in Plowden and Rousseau on individual interests has potentially limiting implications for the curriculum followed by girls, it is conceivable that the *methods* introduced by the liberal progressivists may have been, albeit unwittingly, more girl friendly. The introduction of project work and the fostering of enquiry skills were designed to empower individuals, to involve them in investigations, and to encourage an element of self-directed learning. While such methods were thought likely to benefit all pupils individually, they may have been particularly advantageous for girls. As we shall see in Chapter 5, there has been a steady rise in the level of girls' academic attainment; yet there is also evidence to show that girls get less than their fair share of attention in more conventional teaching situations. So it seems entirely plausible that girls' improved performance is related to the increased provision for individualized learning in schools. For women this may turn out to be one of the more important legacies of the 1960s.

3 Teaching as a female profession

As was pointed out at the beginning of the century by John Dewey (1859–1952) the relations between school and society are two-way: the nature of society influences school; and what is done in school influences society. Only in unusual circumstances can a school effectively remove itself from the prevailing social climate: in Scotland, Kurt Hahn's Gordonstoun, for example, was designed to rescue young people from a defective culture and to fortify them with more appropriate values so that they were immune from its baleful influence on their return. It may make some sense to talk like this in the case of individual boarding schools, but it makes no sense at all in the case of a public system of schooling; ultimately schools and schoolteachers are part of society. Given that sexual inequality is still widespread in our society (EOC, 1993) it is not surprising that such inequalities are also to be found in schools themselves.

In schools, professional roles are unevenly distributed among men and women, much as in the rest of society. Some general markers will be enough at this stage to indicate what we mean. While men and women teachers are present in roughly equal numbers in secondary schools, women are seriously under-represented among headteachers, and in other more senior positions. To reinforce this picture further, most men teachers are in fact to be found in secondary schools. Only 20 per cent of all teachers in English primary schools are men (10 per cent in Scotland), but even here, where male staff are very much in the minority, more than half hold promoted posts. Men are also more likely to be found teaching older

children in primary schools; this is where they have traditionally operated, and where many have chosen to operate
because of perceptions of status and increased responsibility.
Deviating from this pattern can be difficult for a male teacher
who feels this is not where he wants to teach; the teaching of
the youngest pupils in primary schools is generally a difficult
position for men to obtain, and men are well nigh invisible in
the under-fives nursery sector.

So the message is clearly transmitted through universal
schooling to the next generation that working on a day-to-
day basis with younger children, particularly the youngest
children, is women's work, and also that children should
naturally expect to find men in more senior positions of
responsibility in schools. Thus, whilst attempting to foster a
critical awareness of inequalities in society, schools themselves
exhibit an unequal distribution of professional positions.
Wollstonecraft and Mill both pressed for the opening up of all
professional work to women, and at the present time there
remain no formal barriers to the advancement of women in
schools. But as we shall see in more detail in this chapter, and
the chapter following, men and women have not occupied
(and still do not occupy) comparable positions in teaching:
access does not mean equity.

Again, this situation has a history. There can be little doubt
that through time women in teaching have been used and
exploited. Yet in terms of numbers they have been prominent
in teaching as in no other profession. According to Bradley
(1989), in 1851 two-thirds of all teachers in England were
women; and by 1872 this proportion had grown to three-
quarters. Figures for elementary schoolteachers derived by
Apple (1985) from Bergen (1982) suggest that in 1870 half
were women and that by the beginning of the century women
occupied three-quarters of the posts. Even if these two
accounts do not seem entirely consistent, they both serve to
show a steady growth in the relative numerical presence of
women. Figures in Scotland show a similar trend. Today men
constitute one-third of the Scottish teaching profession. A

hundred years ago, this figure was at about 40 per cent. Forty years before that, in the mid-nineteenth century, men made up two-thirds of the teaching profession (Corr, 1983).

The period from 1870 onwards (1872 in Scotland) saw the introduction of compulsory attendance at elementary schools, which brought an increase in the number of schools and the sheer quantity of schooling required. This offered a great opportunity to those interested in going into teaching – an opportunity which was taken up, as the figures show, particularly by women, probably because other comparable jobs such as office work, which was also expanding, were reserved for men. For women, however, the obvious alternatives to teaching were less attractive, not more attractive; and for most of a century, and perhaps up till the present, schoolteaching has been a route for the upward mobility of women, as well as a clear route into employment for women from more middle-class origins. If never the most prestigious of professions, teaching nevertheless offered women a modicum of public standing as well as an outlet for their intelligence. Other work pursued by women was very often of lower status, and failed to provide comparable respectability or challenge. The lack of alternative professional openings, however, undoubtedly made women teachers vulnerable. They were more poorly paid than men, and although this was common practice up until the 1960s, it could be, and was, defended on the grounds that women were not as well qualified. Women, after all, only became admitted to universities at the end of the nineteenth century, and the numbers of female graduates in or out of teaching were minimal until well into the present century. Women were not expected to be as well qualified as men. In Scotland this position was formalized over a long period from 1926 up to the end of the 1960s, during which time virtually all men in the profession, including all male primary teachers, had to possess a university degree.

Historically, the vulnerability of women teachers' position was graphically illustrated by marriage bars which required women to choose between teaching and marrying. This policy was imposed at local authority level, and while some authorities had marriage bars before the First World War, it was the inter-war years which saw this restriction elevated to a norm. Married women could not get a job in teaching, and women who were already teaching knew that if they married they would have to give up their posts. By the 1930s only 10 per cent of women teachers were married (Oram, 1989).

There were two main objections to the employment of married women teachers. The first was that teachers should exhibit model behaviour; and the socially approved ideal required that women should function as home-makers. Ever since the Boer War there had been a perceived need for 'race regeneration'. It was thought that the birth rate was too low, and that women's role was to rear more children. Married teachers were conspicuously neglecting their duty as women by marginalizing their domestic role, and thus setting a bad example to the impressionable young – and perhaps to children's parents as well. Teachers had to be respectable. The working mother was a phenomenon to be associated with factory and other lower-status forms of employment.

The judgemental dimension in this has been well documented. Glasgow's requirement, imposed in 1915, that women resign on marriage allowed temporary reprieve to any whose husband had 'deserted her through no misdemeanour of her own'. This censorious tone was still evident in 1939 when Edinburgh remained hostile to the idea of married women, with or without extant husbands. The Revd Dr Guthrie is minuted as declaring that the Education Committee 'could not become a compassionate society for the employment of widows'; a town councillor pointed out that no one had forced these women teachers to get married, and they ought to remember that they married 'for better or for worse' (Adams, 1990).

This brings in the economic dimension. Because of their social position, married teachers were often seen as not requiring their own income, although Glasgow's marriage bar did exempt women whose husbands were unemployed. And in an era when chronic unemployment extended to the teaching profession itself, young newly trained teachers were in plentiful supply. From the employers' point of view, replacing established, experienced women teachers with younger staff offered the prospect of financial savings, and it was seen by some as only right and proper that married women should be supported by their husbands' earnings.

In parts of America, the mistreatment of women teachers went beyond requiring them to resign on marriage: even the most innocent relationships with the opposite sex had to be avoided. Private lives were regulated, as in these stipulations from a contract which teachers in a Southern state were required to sign:

> I promise to abstain from all dancing, immodest dressing, and any other conduct unbecoming a teacher and a lady.

> I promise not to go out with any young men except in so far as it may be necessary to stimulate Sunday-school work.

> I promise not to fall in love, to become engaged or *secretly married*.

> (Waller, 1932, p. 43, italics added)

In reacting to this, we have to remember that total discretion over one's private life is a right which has only recently achieved widespread acceptance. Until relatively late on, bank clerks were forbidden to marry until they were twenty-five, and nurses in hospital residences had their leisure hours and social lives controlled in a way that would be unacceptable today.

In the 1920s there was certainly opposition to the marriage bar from married women teachers, but the general response of those who wished to stay in the profession was one which may not have altogether suited the authorities: women teachers stayed single, creating a long-lasting image which has faded only recently – the woman teacher as dedicated spinster. Thus, by the 1930s, women still made up the clear majority of the teaching profession, but only one in ten of these women teachers were married. In some senses, teaching provided women with a 'choice' between career and marriage, and with the financial means which made it possible to remain single. Given the choice between teaching and a husband, a significant number of women teachers felt they had too much to lose by getting married. Any kind of job was hard to come by, but for women to acquire some status and professional identity was an achievement, and one to be valued. This is what teaching offered, and women were unwilling to give it up. They certainly had no need of a meal ticket, for however modest their salaries, they were sufficient to allow these women to maintain a respectable independence. For many, teaching represented a step up the social ladder. Throughout the first half of this century large numbers of recruits to the teaching profession have come from non-professional backgrounds. Teachers whose fathers were manual workers were to be found at their most significant levels in primary schools – the sector where there has also been the highest concentration of women (Floud and Scott, 1961).

The inter-war period was one where the supply of teachers was greater than the number of jobs available in schools. It will be useful to contrast this with the 1960s situation where the demand for teachers outstripped the supply. Because of an earlier growth in the birth rate, there were more children in the system. And because of changing ideas about education there was held to be a need to reduce the size of classes. These two factors together created an explosion of demand for teachers to which the government responded primarily by expanding teacher training. In Scotland, three additional colleges of education were built. In England, the numbers of teachers-in-training more than doubled during the 1960s, although the extension of non-graduate training from two years to three years at the start of the decade made it more difficult to produce more trained teachers quickly.

With marriage bars outlawed since the end of the Second World War, however, a less expensive option suggested itself.

Running alongside the expansion of teacher training, a campaign was mounted to encourage back to the classroom qualified women teachers who had left their posts in order to have children and to bring up families. Authorities and head-teachers went out of their way to make it 'easy' for women teachers to return, with their young children being given priority admission to nursery classes so that the mothers were then available to teach. Evetts (1990) interviewed a group of primary headteachers who had taken breaks in service in the 1960s, at an earlier stage in their careers. These women tended to have re-entered teaching sooner than they had planned, usually because they were approached by someone they knew, often a former colleague. Some felt they could now do the job better because of their intimate experience of young children, and contact had often been maintained with education through occasional supply teaching. Where they did express concerns and anxieties was over whether they could combine school and family; but the official view was that women in this position should be given every support and encouragement. Today, however, the return of experienced women teachers to the profession after a significant break in service may be more problematic. The pace of change in education has accelerated to the point where returning to teaching may be much more difficult.

This interest in the 1960s in actively recruiting married women represented a remarkable change in attitude from the oppressive model of vocation which was formalized in the marriage bar; but the needs of the system have a wonderful way of relaxing such restrictive notions, which can only be maintained where there is a ready supply of alternative, and more acceptable, labour. Where teachers are scarce, such a model becomes untenable. Looking back over more than a century, we can see that when more teachers are required (post-1870 and the 1960s) women are drafted in. When there are too many teachers (1920s and 1930s) women are put under pressure to leave. The first scenario encourages women to see themselves as being there to fill the gaps; the second

49

scenario suggests that they are fortunate if they are able to hold on to their jobs.

This historical perspective suggests that we have indeed made some progress. It would now be unthinkable to require women to relinquish their posts – or would it? Today the most vulnerable groups are part-time or temporary or occasional teachers: one in eight of all female staff in Scotland currently come into these categories. Where a school roll falls, some of these jobs will be the first to go. Part-time work, however, suits many women in the sense that such jobs allow child care and job commitments to be combined. Women have argued for yet more flexible work practices and conditions; for example, job sharing has been developed as a means of offering full-time posts. But such positions, particularly in the eyes of managers, tend to make their occupants peripheral, and seen as less-committed teachers.

Oram (1989) suggests that in the 1920s and 1930s women teachers were criticized whatever their marital status. If they were single, they were portrayed as professional spinsters – unattractive, obsessive, blinkered, and odd. Married teachers were seen as greedy for a second salary and neglectful of their domestic duties. When married women came into teaching in significant numbers after the Second World War, they were often seen by their own single colleagues, as well as by male colleagues, as inevitably less committed to their jobs because they also had family lives and commitments.

Given this cultural and institutional tradition of discriminating against women, Casey and Apple (1989) argue that teaching as a profession suffers at the hands of those in power at least partly because teaching is a 'female' profession, as has also been suggested for other areas of professional employment for women, such as nursing and social work. This may be particularly true of the primary education sector, since this is the sphere where there is the greatest concentration of women. In Scotland almost two-thirds of women teachers work in primary schools, but only 13 per cent of male teachers work in this sector. It is significant that primary teaching is seen by some as an occupation with lower status than secondary teaching. The great majority of graduates from the traditional university sector are to be found in the secondary schools. Much of the material in a primary school curriculum is seemingly familiar to many parents, whilst the specialisms of the secondary school curriculum deal with material which is seen to be more advanced, and which may appear as inaccessible to most parents. The child-centred philosophy embraced by many primary schools may itself have contributed to misperceptions of primary school teachers' work as undemanding. In this approach the teacher is cast as a facilitator of learning rather than as an authority who imparts knowledge directly.

While it is true that for a decade or more the teaching profession as a whole has been portrayed by government as often misguided in its methods, it is clear that much of this criticism has been levelled particularly at primary teachers. In this sector there is seen to be a failure to teach the basics. The present government is unhappy about progressive child-centred methods of learning which it sees as having dominated thinking in primary schools for far too long. It is argued that there is a need to return to a system where the core elements of the curriculum are clearly stated, and where pupil performance is assessed in a rigorous and systematic way. No other professional group, with the possible exception of social workers, has been subject to so much criticism in recent years, from the government, the media, and the public. Interestingly, elementary school teachers and social workers are grouped together, along with librarians and nurses, in Amitai Etzioni's famous collection of discussions of *The Semi-Professions and their Organization* (1969), which notes the prevalence of women in these posts. One essay patronizingly claims of women: 'Their low work commitment makes some women welcome an easy job that makes few demands, and it is easier to follow instructions than to exercise judgment' (Simpson and Simpson, 1969, p. 231). If there is any truth in this, it is that many women occupy subordinate positions in

professional hierarchies, and in such positions it is often difficult to do anything other than to conform to expectations.
This is not a deficiency on the part of women, however, but
the result of attitudes and institutional structures which effectively discriminate against women in the workplace, and
elsewhere in society. To give an illustration, applying for
promotion whilst pregnant may present a real dilemma for
some women. First, would most women even consider applying if they were pregnant? If a woman does apply, and she
reveals that she is pregnant, is it likely that she will be
appointed? Would she even be considered as a 'serious' candidate for interview? On the other hand, if she applies, keeps
quiet, and accepts the job, what will her professional standing
be? Pregnancy may be a handicap to promotion, as this
example suggests, but in real terms the *prospect* of pregnancy
is more likely to be viewed as a handicap, whatever the formal
position as defined in policy statements from employers and
by government legislation.

Ironically, a principal reason why primary teaching has
traditionally been regarded as suitable work for women may
be exactly because one of the roles expected of women in our
society is the care of the young. For women who function
both as teachers and as parents at the same time, however,
there is potentially a double problem, with feelings of in-
adequacy generated by the failure to be either the ideal parent
or the wholly successful teacher. Each role competes in terms
of time and energy with the other. As Julia Evetts notes in her
study of primary teachers: 'Guilt was the inevitable conse-
quence' (Evetts, 1990, p. 131). But to return to the present
government's disquiet about teaching methods in schools,
primary teachers would appear to be particularly distrusted
over method, as opposed to content, since content can be
determined centrally by the implementation of a national
curriculum. While officially seeing questions of method in
primary teaching as beyond governmental competence, the
Education Secretary appointed three hand-picked educationists at the end of 1991 to pronounce on this. They did what

they were required to do: they criticized the progressive approach which had been advocated by Plowden and adopted by many primary teachers; and they extolled whole-class teaching (Alexander *et al.*, 1992). The ideas and the practice of many primary teachers, and their professional competence, thus became publicly devalued. And almost grotesquely, the three people who professed to know better were all men – a professor, a chief inspector, and an educational bureaucrat – judging a sector of education where the great majority of teaching staff are women. As far as the professions are concerned, for example the legal or medical professions, it is much harder to imagine a male-dominated occupational group allowing its own thinking to be denigrated, its views overruled, and its practice dictated in such an intrusive way.

Again, similar points could be argued in relation to other occupational groups – nursing, for example – where many women are employed. These occupations have not tradition-ally enjoyed the same high status as other professions, as is shown by the label 'the semi-professional'; and they have a demonstrable history of subordination, as is shown by the marriage bars common to both teaching and nursing. The experiences of women in teaching over the last century, and up to the present time, would therefore suggest the following picture: women teachers are subject to the lower status of women in society generally, to the lower status of teaching as compared to other professions, to the lower status of the nursery and primary sectors as compared to the secondary sector, and to the lower status associated with part-time or temporary employment. In the next chapter we will look at the *current* position of women in teaching, since the advent of equal opportunities employers and policies.

4 Teaching and promoted posts

In the previous chapter it was shown that women have traditionally occupied a subordinate position within teaching, a fact which clearly raises questions about whether schools constitute a credible, let alone an effective, environment for promoting sexual equality. In this chapter we examine in more detail current patterns of gender inequalities within the teaching profession, with particular reference to levels of promotion.

In the broadest terms, many more men than women are in powerful positions. This should concern us for a variety of reasons. In the school system a great many decisions, large and small, are being taken by people who see the world from a male point of view. For example, the majority of people who determine which teachers will be promoted are men who have already been promoted; it is entirely likely that they think the people most fit for promotion are those who most closely resemble themselves.

Further, the maldistribution of men and women staff seems bound to convey undesirable messages. Pupils see that it is the (almost) invariable order of things that large institutions are run by men. In secondary schools, which have often prided themselves on being meritocratic institutions, the role model implications for thousands of pupils are worrying. If for no other reason, secondary schools might be better places if many more women occupied senior management positions. In Scotland at the beginning of the present decade, for example, out of 415 local authority secondary schools, there were only 11 women headteachers (SOED, 1992). In primary schools, where there are men in post, more often than not they are in positions of special responsibility. Again, this clearly has the potential to convey a powerful message to children. It is not, after all, uncommon for the only male member of staff in a primary school to be the headteacher; in this situation a male headteacher is seen presiding over a group made up exclusively of female class teachers, with all that that may signify.

Such concern with role models (and with mentors) is not only confined to pupils. Some young female teachers may see the existing distribution of posts as indicating the limits to which they can reasonably aspire. Men receive very different messages, and their expectations are consequently high. So much so, in fact, that these can become feelings of entitlement. One study (Strathclyde Department of Education, 1988) found that male primary teachers who failed to achieve promotion were driven to explain this in terms of a new discrimination against men; promotion for men in primary education had come to be seen as a *legitimate* expectation, a notion clearly derived from the traditional pattern of men in promoted posts and of women in subordinate positions.

However, the most fundamental objection to the relative position of men and women in teaching is simply one of inequity. This can be seen at its most basic in terms of salaries. Differences in salary are obviously related to differences in level of post, and these in turn may (so it is often suggested) be related to continuity in service. We now turn to some evidence.

To start with, we may make a crude distinction between teachers who have been promoted and teachers who have not. The 'unpromoted' category includes those who have failed to achieve promotion, have no wish for promotion, and have joined the teaching profession so recently that the question of promotion has not arisen. The 'promoted' category includes people from a wide variety of grades from the most senior to teachers who have just been elevated above the basic grade. The position of basic grade is increasingly referred to in the new managerialist climate as that of an 'ordinary class teacher' – an epithet which underlines a conception of success-fulness as necessarily involving elevation from the ranks.

The promotion structure has of recent years assumed increasing importance for three reasons. First, the pace of educational change has accelerated, with most of it initiated from the centre. The model for communicating innovation to teachers which is currently favoured is the 'cascade': one teacher in a senior post from each school attends a briefing session, and these teachers then brief other teachers in (say) their subject departments. Second, the political climate has transmitted to schools the importance of management, and therefore the importance of those in a position to manage. In a line management structure, there is an explicit frame of reference: whatever your position, you know to whom you are answerable, and who is answerable to you. Only unpromoted teachers have no one answering to them, except pupils.

Table 4.1: Representation of women teachers by promotion and type of school. *Sources*: SOED Statistics, 1992 and DFE Statistics, 1993.

Percentage of teachers who are women (%)	Scotland[a]		England and Wales[b]	
Number of teachers who are women (n =)	September 1990 (in education authority schools)		March 1991 (in maintained schools)	
	Nursery and Primary	Secondary	Nursery and Primary	Secondary
Promoted teachers[c,d]	83%	34%	73%	43%
	5,242	4,551	70,694	60,248
Unpromoted teachers	95%	62%	90%	61%
	16,389	6,514	73,601	36,663
All teachers	92%	46%	81%	48%
	21,634	11,065	144,295	96,911

[a] percentages and numbers are based on full-time equivalents of teachers in service
[b] percentages and numbers are based on full-time teachers in service
[c] promoted staff are senior, assistant principal and principal teacher; and assistant head, deputy head, and head teachers
[d] promoted staff are on the main scale with incentive allowance, or deputy and headteachers

If this tends to depress the status of the 'ordinary' class teacher, so too does the *proliferation* of promoted posts, which over the last two decades has produced a secondary school career structure which differs markedly from the relatively 'flat' pattern of the primary school. Staff who hold promoted positions are clearly better placed to define the needs of schools for others; and they also have a vested interest in emphasizing the importance and status associated with such elevated positions. At the most general level, Table 4.1 provides an overview of the position of women teachers within the promotion structures of both primary and secondary schools. While women are in the minority in secondary schools (as a group they represent 48 per cent of full-time secondary teachers in England and Wales, and 46 per cent in Scotland) they constitute the majority in the unpromoted category (61 per cent in England and Wales, and 62 per

Table 4.2: Percentage distribution across grade by type of school, graduate status and gender. Full-time teachers in maintained nursery, primary and secondary schools in England and Wales, 1991.
Source: DFE Statistics, 1993.

Row percentage (%)	Head teachers	Deputy Head teachers	Main scale plus incentive allowance					Main scale no allowance	All teachers (n = 100%)
			E	D	C	B	A		
Nursery and primary									
Non-graduates[a]									
Women	9%	10%	0%	0%	1%	15%	18%	47%	92,938
Men	39%	20%	0%	1%	2%	14%	7%	17%	18,922
Graduates									
Women	5%	6%	0%	0%	1%	13%	17%	58%	51,357
Men	23%	18%	0%	1%	2%	14%	12%	30%	15,033
Secondary									
Non-graduates[a]									
Women	1%	3%	2%	9%	8%	27%	14%	36%	37,623
Men	3%	4%	5%	18%	10%	27%	9%	24%	31,970
Graduates									
Women	1%	4%	2%	9%	8%	22%	15%	39%	59,288
Men	4%	8%	7%	19%	10%	20%	9%	23%	71,133

[a] including graduate equivalents

cent in Scotland). Women are under-represented in promoted positions in primary schools also.

Looking at the English figures in more detail (see Table 4.2) we see that graduate status appears to have little overall effect on the relative chances of men and women, although this picture may change as graduates come to represent a greater proportion of new recruits to the profession. However, the current situation does not suggest that this is likely to happen. In the primary sector, the chances of men – whether graduates or non-graduates – achieving primary headships are between four and five times greater than the chances of women teachers with comparable qualifications. Scale B is achieved by similar proportions of male and female staff. (There are very few posts at Grades C to E in primary schools.) For secondary headships the disparities are also very marked, among both graduates and non-graduates. As we move through grades towards more senior positions of responsibility in secondary schools, men begin to overtake

Table 4.3: Representation of women secondary teachers by main teaching subject. Full-time equivalents of teachers in education authority secondary schools in Scotland, 1990.
Source: SOED Statistics, 1992.

Percentage who are women (%)	Subject		Subject		Subject	
Number who are women (n =)	Home Economics	100% 1,321	Physical Education	47% 755	History	34% 403
	Modern Languages	78% 1,210	Biology	46% 551	Modern Studies	29% 157
	Business Studies	76% 832	Mathematics	42% 1,164	Chemistry	22% 317
	Englsh	60% 1,815	Art	40% 575	Physics	14% 161
	Music	56% 424%	Computing	37% 150	Technological Education	1% 8
	Religious Education	47% 183	Geography	35% 429		

women at Grade C, and by Grade D the gap has greatly widened.

Table 4.1 provides a clear reminder of how few men teach in the primary sector. But while numbers of males and females teaching in secondary schools are much more comparable, within secondary schools there are further marked disparities between different school subjects (see Table 4.3). That home economics is taught exclusively by women, while technological education is (almost) exclusively taught by men is perhaps unsurprising. Figures based on Scotland, however, show that these imbalances are not confined to such subjects. The over-representation of women teachers is also marked in business studies, modern languages and English departments, whilst women are relatively poorly represented in social sciences departments, and in chemistry and physics departments. There are some exceptions, with broadly equal numbers of female and male staff in biology, mathematics, and physical education. Thus, it is not only in terms of promoted posts that women are under-represented, but their absence is also notable within particular areas of the secondary school curriculum.

Again looking at a more detailed and focused picture, this time from Grampian region, we can see that the numerical predominance of women within a subject area is not reflected in their occupancy of the post of principal teacher (head of subject department). The subject areas listed in Table 4.4 correspond to the different modes of the curriculum within which subjects are taught to pupils in the first four years of secondary schooling in Scotland. The first three subject areas listed in the table are taught by more women than men, and yet the predominance of women in these subject areas is no more likely to affect their chances of promotion than else-where in the school. In modern languages, for example, there are almost twice as many female staff as male; yet only 17 per cent of these women are principal teachers compared with 60 per cent of the men. The data presented in Table 4.4 clearly show that men are much more likely than women to occupy

Table 4.4: Percentage distribution of secondary teachers across grade by main teaching subject area and gender. Full-time equivalents of teachers in education authority secondary schools in Grampian Region, Scotland, 1992.
Source: GRCED Statistics, 1992.

Row percentage (%)	Principal teacher	Assistant principal teacher	Senior teacher	Teacher	Principal teacher (guidance)	All teachers (*n* =)
English						
Women	6%	11%	14%	59%	10%	144
Men	31%	5%	17%	31%	16%	90
Modern Languages						
Women	17%	3%	13%	63%	4%	161
Men	60%	4%	4%	28%	4%	83
Mathematics						
Women	5%	12%	13%	65%	5%	116
Men	30%	10%	9%	40%	11%	103
Technological Activities						
Women	28%	2%	7%	60%	3%	190
Men	29%	7%	8%	43%	13%	191
Scientific Studies						
Women	10%	–	9%	71%	10%	113
Men	50%	5%	7%	31%	7%	201
Environmental and Social Studies						
Women	23%	2%	11%	51%	13%	79
Men	57%	3%	5%	22%	13%	161
Aesthetic and Creative Activities						
Women	23%	2%	8%	65%	3%	113
Men	54%	5%	7%	32%	2%	127
Religious Education						
Women	53%	5%	–	42%	-	19
Men	63%	3%	–	34%	–	35
Physical Education						
Women	11%	2%	11%	62%	14%	62
Men	48%	6%	10%	22%	16%	63

the position of principal teacher in almost all subject areas, right across the secondary school curriculum. There are two exceptions: technological activities and religious education. In the case of technological activities, the data mask a clear division of teachers into 'all female' and 'all male' departments

Table 4.5: Percentage distribution across grade by type of school, gender, and age. Full-time equivalents of teachers in education authority nursery, primary and secondary schools in Scotland, 1990.
Source: SOED Statistics, 1992.

Column percentage (%)	Age group									All teachers
	< 25	25–29	30–34	35–39	40–44	45–49	50–54	55–59	≥ 60	
Nursery and primary										
Women										
Head Teacher	–	1%	4%	6%	9%	13%	14%	16%	17%	9%
Deputy/Assistant	–	1%	4%	5%	6%	8%	11%	10%	8%	6%
Senior Teacher	–	4%	14%	11%	11%	10%	9%	6%	4%	10%
Teacher	100%	94%	78%	78%	74%	69%	66%	68%	71%	75%
All (n =100%)	1,106	1,614	2,202	4,267	4,618	3,129	2,595	1,675	426	21,634
Men										
Head Teacher	–	2%	12%	32%	46%	48%	53%	60%	43%	38%
Deputy/Assistant	–	2%	9%	11%	8%	12%	9%	4%	5%	8%
Senior Teacher	–	3%	16%	17%	9%	8%	2%	2%	2%	9%
Teacher	100%	93%	63%	40%	37%	31%	36%	34%	50%	45%
All (n = 100%)	46	113	186	447	404	201	206	178	116	1,897
Secondary										
Women										
Head Teacher	–	–	–	–	0%	0%	0%	0%	0%	0%[a]
Deputy/Assistant	–	–	0%	2%	3%	3%	3%	5%	5%	2%
Principal	1%	5%	14%	20%	21%	26%	27%	29%	27%	19%
Assistant Principal	2%	9%	12%	13%	12%	12%	12%	14%	13%	12%
Senior Teacher	–	3%	10%	9%	9%	9%	8%	8%	5%	8%
Teacher	97%	83%	64%	56%	55%	50%	48%	44%	48%	59%
All (n = 100%)	301	1,185	1,774	2,390	2,315	1,512	963	517	106	11,065
Men										
Head Teacher	–	–	–	0%	2%	5%	8%	9%	6%	3%
Deputy/Assistant	–	–	1%	6%	11%	13%	16%	13%	12%	9%
Principal	–	7%	22%	37%	47%	49%	47%	44%	39%	39%
Assistant Principal	1%	6%	13%	16%	14%	12%	10%	11%	10%	13%
Senior Teacher	–	4%	9%	8%	4%	2%	1%	1%	1%	4%
Teacher	99%	83%	55%	33%	22%	19%	18%	22%	32%	32%
All (n = 100%)	114	616	1,504	2,721	3,271	1,921	1,497	916	362	12,923

[a] in total, 11 women headteachers of Scottish education authority secondary schools

(i.e. home economics and 'technical' departments). In other words, at the extreme, there are no male staff to promote in a home economics department. Religious education is also exceptional because of the small number of staff involved (one or two teachers in each of the region's schools). Thus, women are under-represented in promoted posts, not only in the school as a whole, but also within almost every subject department of the secondary school.

Table 4.5 shows the different ages by which men and women have established themselves in different grades in Scottish schools. In this table perhaps the most instructive horizontal lines to read are the ones marked 'teacher'. Up to the age of 30, in both primary and secondary schools, similar numbers of men and women have achieved some degree of promotion. (At this stage there are evidently better prospects for promotion in secondary schools than there are in primary schools, since secondary schools have a higher proportion of promoted posts.) From the age of 30 onwards, however, the proportion of men remaining at the basic grade becomes progressively smaller than the proportion of women. The same general patterns of career progression are observed if the horizontal lines at the opposite end of the promotion scale are read (where senior management positions within the school are marked in the table as 'head' and 'deputy/assistant'). Teachers' salaries in England and Wales tell a similar story with no significant difference between men and women until after the age of 30, but with a consistent gap between average male and female earnings beyond that point (see Table 4.6).

Sikes *et al.* (1985) detect an 'age 30' transition in their study of teachers' careers. They also note a 'pronounced'

Table 4.6: Average salary by type of school, gender and age. Full-time teachers in maintained nursery, primary, and secondary schools in England and Wales, 1991.
Source: DFE Statistics, 1993.

Average salary (x £1,000)	Age group									All teachers (n = 100%)
	< 25	25–29	30–34	35–39	40–44	45–49	50–54	55–59	≥ 60	
Nursery and primary										
Women	11k	13k	15k	16k	16k	17k	18k	18k	18k	144,295
Men	11k	13k	17k	18k	19k	20k	20k	20k	20k	33,955
Secondary										
Women	11k	13k	16k	17k	17k	18k	19k	19k	19k	96,911
Men	11k	13k	17k	18k	19k	20k	21k	21k	20k	103,103

Table 4.7: Movement of teachers by gender and age, 1990–1. Full-time teachers under 50 years of age in maintained nursery, primary, and secondary schools in England and Wales.
Source: DFE Statistics, 1993.

As a percentage of full-time teachers (%)	Age group						All movements under 50 years ($n = $)
	< 25	25–29	30–34	35–39	40–44	45–49	
Women							
Leavers[a]	10%	13%	13%	8%	7%	6%	16,634
Re-entrants[b]	0%	3%	6%	9%	8%	4%	11,869
Men							
Leavers[a]	11%	11%	6%	4%	4%	4%	5,751
Re-entrants[b]	0%	3%	2%	2%	2%	1%	1,984

[a] excluding transfers out, and expressed as percentage of full-time teachers in service at beginning of year

[b] excluding transfers in, and expressed as percentage of full-time teachers in service at end of the year

gender effect at this stage. After a period of initial socialization, male teachers show a 'new-found urgency' in promotion and management issues. For some men perceptions of growing family commitments place earnings and promotion at the top of the agenda, whilst for some women an awareness of a 'dual career' has grown, with the sense that the choice is now between family and job. The data presented in Table 4.7 would appear to confirm this picture of age 30 as a significant transitional point in career trajectories, since it marks a point at which women and men leave teaching at very different rates. Before this point there is a 1 in 10 drop-out rate for both men and women. Women in their thirties, however, are twice as likely to leave teaching as men in their thirties. Significant numbers of men as well as women at some point re-enter teaching for a further spell of service, but this is much more likely to be the case amongst women.

The patterning of economic activity by gender and age is not peculiar to the teaching profession. More generally, among the female workforce in Britain, economic activity rates rise to a peak around age 30, and then show a marked

Table 4.8: Representation of women teachers by type of school and mode of
employment. Full-time equivalents of teachers in education authority
primary and secondary schools in Scotland, 1990.
Source: SOED Statistics, 1992.

Percentage of teachers who are women (%) *Number of teachers who are women* (n =)	Mode of employment				
	Full-time permanent	Full-time temporary	Part-time permanent	Part-time temporary	Occasional
Primary	90%	96%	99%	99%	97%
	18,281	967	566	554	378
Secondary	43%	75%	95%	94%	78%
	9,503	545	366	410	238

decline, only to recover around age 45 (EOC, 1993). The
statistics show that these patterns of female employment are
clearly related to the care of dependent children, and also that
many women who remain economically active throughout
their thirties work in part-time jobs, combining employment
with child-care responsibilities. The relevance of this for
women teachers is emphasized by the data shown in Table
4.8. In both the primary and secondary sectors, women are
much more likely than men to be in part-time or temporary
employment. In Scottish schools, around one in twelve
women teachers are employed on a part-time or occasional
basis. Thus, it is not only in terms of 'career breaks' that the
picture is markedly different for men and women, but also in
terms of mode of employment. In more ways than one, therefore, a significant number of women teachers may come to
occupy what are perceived as more marginal or peripheral
positions in schools, at a time when many of their peers are
focused on career development and promotion.

We can use this information about career trajectories to
illuminate the question of promotion to headships. In the
primary sector the numbers of women entering the profession
suggest that women should be well placed to occupy the great
majority of primary headships. In England, where more than

fourth-fifths of primary staff are female, women hold less than one-half of these senior posts. In Scotland, where only one in ten primary staff are male, men hold one-third of primary headships, while women hold two-thirds. These figures, however, while disquieting in their own right, mask more significant inequities.

The category of 'primary head' includes posts which vary widely in scope, responsibility, and salary. An examination of Grampian region illustrates the differences (Darling and Glendinning, 1993). In terms of size, the region's primary schools range from a single-teacher school with fewer than 10 pupils to the largest school with a roll well in excess of 700 pupils. Both schools have heads, and in a census each head counts as one; yet the jobs are so different that it could be questioned whether it is meaningful to include both under the same statistical heading. Investigation revealed that where women occupied more senior management positions in primary schools, these were likely to be in smaller schools with a smaller management team.

Because there is a large, sparsely populated area in the region, the majority of primary schools were in fact 'small' schools where the headteachers also took responsibility for teaching a class, although a relief teacher released the head in order to create some time for administrative tasks. Of the headteachers who were also teaching 73 per cent were women. By contrast, in schools where the headteacher did not teach, and where there were also other promoted staff at the level of deputy or assistant headteacher, only 52 per cent of headteachers were women.

Differences in the distribution of male and female primary headteachers were also related to the size of the school roll (see Table 4.9). More than half of the female heads were in charge of small schools (100 pupils or less), while only a quarter of female heads in the region were in charge of large schools (with more than 220 pupils). Male heads were more evenly distributed over the full range of schools. On average, female primary headteachers were responsible for 145 pupils,

Table 4.9: Percentage distribution of primary headteachers by size of school and
gender. Education authority primary schools in Grampian Region,
Scotland, 1992.
Source: GRCED Statistics, 1992.

Row percentage (%)	Size of primary school roll				
	≤ 100 pupils	101–220 pupils	221–500 pupils	> 500 pupils	All primary headteachers (n =)
Women	52%	23%	24%	1%	179
Men	32%	31%	33%	4%	95

whereas their male counterparts were responsible for 197
pupils. This has clear implications for the salaries of male and
female heads.

Similar findings emerged from a study of an English LEA
(Hill, 1994). The smallest primary schools had equal numbers
of male heads and female heads. Women occupied the majority
of headships in medium-sized schools (Group 4). But only 20
per cent of the heads of the largest schools (Group 7) were
women. According to Hill, appointments to these well-paid
positions are usually made from those who have experience of
managing smaller schools. Career trajectories suggest that the
relative inaccessibility for women of headships of large schools
may be a reflection of the fact that the women heads had tended
to get their first headships later than the men. This was particularly so for those women who had taken a break in service.
Significantly none of the women heads who had entered teaching after 1970 had taken such a break. While this may have
given them an advantage over women whose teaching career
had not been continuous, this strategy is not a solution to
achieving equal opportunities with men, since even this group
of women obtained their headships later than the men.

In secondary schools, the problem is exacerbated by the
multi-layered promotion structure. In Scotland in the 1970s
additional ranks were introduced, and it became the norm to
advance through these ranks one by one until such time as

one's progress came to a halt. Similarly in England, the salary structure has developed in a way that has produced more levels of promotedness. To get to the top of a secondary school requires a significant number of steps; for most, this can only be accomplished over a substantial period of time. We have seen that women teachers move into promoted posts more slowly and therefore later. This, together with their earlier age of retirement, means that they have a relatively short period in which to ascend the ladder.

One relevant consideration here is the level of women's ambitiousness. Some want to use as an explanation of women's relative absence from top teaching posts the view that women are not so effectively socialized into being ambitious or competitive. An NUT study in 1980, however, clearly demonstrated that many women *did* want promotion. Some light may be shed on this uncertain area by considering the level of applications for promoted posts. A useful study here is the investigation of promotion and gender conducted by the largest education authority in Europe – Strathclyde Region.

The Strathclyde research focused on appointments made over a limited period, from August 1985 to February 1987. Results are presented in the working party's report, *Sex Equality in the Education Service* (1988). How did men and women fare in the promotion stakes during the period investigated? Table 4.10 summarizes the central findings presented in the report. As a lead-in to reading this table, it may be useful to look at a single horizontal line, say the line labelled 'secondary principal teacher or assistant principal teacher'. Here 34 per cent of the applicants were women and (supplying an invisible figure) 66 per cent were men. But although 66 per cent of the applicants were men, only 52 per cent of the jobs went to men. By contrast women constituted 34 per cent of the applicants and got 48 per cent of the jobs.

This is one instance of a general pattern made explicit by the report. The proportion of women on the short leet is higher than the proportion of women among applicants; and the proportion of women among appointments is even higher.

Table 4.10: Appointments to promoted posts in Strathclyde Region, 1985–7.
Source: SRCED, 1988.

Percentage who are women (%) Number who are women (n =)	Of all applicants	Of persons short-leeted	Of persons appointed
Nursery headteacher	97%	96%	100%
	173	51	9
Primary headteacher	61%	75%	85%
	2,810	549	114
Primary assistant headteacher	75%	86%	89%
	2,917	522	85
Secondary headteacher	2%	4%	6%
	9	4	1
Secondary deputy headteacher or assistant headteacher	10%	12%	17%
	461	61	14
Secondary principal teacher or assistant principal teacher	34%	42%	48%
	4,971	743	149
All promoted posts[a]	40%	51%	56%
	11,554	2,027	394

[a] includes various promoted posts in special education

What is noteworthy is that this pattern of rising proportions (henceforth PRP) holds good at all levels (with the possible exception of short-leeted applicants for nursery headships).

Although PRP holds good for all levels of appointment, however, this must not be allowed to obscure significant differences between the levels. If we look now at the appointments to primary headships, we see that women constituted 61 per cent of the applicants, but won 85 per cent of the jobs: while men made up 39 per cent of the applicants and got only 15 per cent of the appointments. This only sounds remarkable until a fresh statistical baseline is introduced: women at this time constituted 92 per cent of the primary teaching profession in Strathclyde. So women were becoming primary heads roughly (though not quite) in accordance with their numerical presence in primary schools.

If we compare this with the situation in Strathclyde secondary schools, a different picture emerges. Women make up less than half the secondary teaching profession, but during the period monitored women teachers accounted for only one out of eighteen new heads. This points to one rough distinction that needs to be drawn (but which is not made in the Strathclyde report) which can be put crudely by saying that during this period women were doing all right in primary schools, but not in secondary schools.

The Strathclyde study, however, noting the unsatisfactory picture of promotion for women in general, offers an all-purpose explanation in terms of job applications.

> The relative absence of women from promoted posts must be attributed to their lesser incidence of application.

> Women applicants were almost twice as likely to be appointed as male applicants.

> If the proportion of women in promoted posts is to be increased, it will evidently be necessary to overcome their reluctance to apply.
> (Strathclyde Department of Education, 1988, pp. 24–5)

This diagnosis certainly seems relevant to the most senior promoted posts in secondary schools: at the secondary head-teacher level with 9 women and 108 men applying for 18 jobs, the need for more female applicants is clear. One difficulty is that the best position from which to apply for a headship is a deputy headship; but there were only about thirty deputy heads in the whole of Scotland at this time. And applications from women for deputy headteacher posts in Strathclyde were not very numerous either.

The shortage of women applicants at this level is a serious problem, but it is also a specific problem. At most levels there are many female applicants. The Strathclyde survey shows that 48 assistant headteacher jobs in secondary schools attracted 422 female applicants, while at the primary head-teacher level 2,810 women applied for 134 jobs. In such substantial trawls, there must be many talented, but unsuccessful, women candidates. There seems to be a naive assumption that a greater number of applications from women would result in a greater number of women being appointed to these posts. It is entirely possible that the outcome would be that there would be a similar number of women getting these jobs, but a greater number of unsuccessful women candidates.

One way to explain the lesser incidence of applications from women would be to surmise that women are less likely to apply for promoted posts unless they are really strong, credible candidates. Instead of worrying about why 92 per cent of Strathclyde's primary staff (the women) were responsible for only 61 per cent of the applications, might one not better ask why 8 per cent (the men) generate 39 per cent of the applications? Here indeed there is disparity, but surely not one to be explained in terms of female deficiencies (such as lack of confidence, or lack of awareness of the opportunities). Instead we need to be able to explain why men, probably including some relatively untalented men, clamour for promotion. Possible answers are not hard to find. Men have traditionally been seen as bearing the main burden of a family's economy. And there is perhaps more pressure on them to be 'successful'; many may have been ineradicably socialized into competitive careerism. When men see a ladder, their conditioned response is to try to climb up.

The remedy advocated in the Strathclyde report is to implement policies which encourage more women to apply for promoted posts. One effect of such a prescription may be to promote competitive careerism as a norm. For many, of course, 'getting on' is an end in itself. But beyond this, it is often argued that having your hands on the instruments of power gives more job satisfaction because it allows you more control over your conditions of work or allows you to 'shape future developments'; negatively, it prevents someone else being the one who tells you what to do. It is questionable whether this argument makes so much sense in the context of teaching, for many schools are in reality a combination of a hierarchical chain of command and a co-operative of independent professionals. Teachers may feel that they establish their real identity in the classroom, where they have considerable discretion over how they teach, and also some discretion over what they teach. In practice, even headteachers can often only make decisions on the day-to-day running of the school, which includes, the management of budgets, allied to a growing number of administrative tasks. The major educational policy decisions are increasingly made elsewhere. In such an environment it would be unwise to construe a lack of interest in applying for promotion as necessarily a pathological condition.

It has been argued elsewhere that the social acceptance and approval of ambition (note the criticism implicit in the phrase 'lack of ambition') is an example of how the culture of a patriarchal society legitimates male attitudes, values and behaviour at the expense of women (see Grant, 1989). One does not have to accept this line of thought, however, to recognize in the Strathclyde research an instance of a now familiar form of argument in the field of gender issues. Where there is an identifiable difference between male behaviour and female behaviour, the male pattern is assumed to be the norm, while the female behaviour is seen as deviant and problematic: it must either change or be changed. While some women are keen to compete (and to encourage others to compete) in the struggle for promotion, others may reject the values underlying male career patterns. Middleton (1989) interviewed one teacher who 'felt that women's mothering role gave them a certain moral superiority over men, whose career patterns and socialization for masculinity deprived them of the opportunity for reflection on moral issues and interpersonal relationships' (p. 61). While there is certainly more to life than promotion, it perhaps ought to be possible to implement a career structure – for women and for men – which acknowledges both ambition

71

and the more personal dimensions in one's life.

The fact that women are relatively few among applicants for the top jobs in secondary schools should occasion little surprise. As with other positions which have long tended to be held by men, such jobs can only be pursued by women who are not easily daunted. A woman who becomes head of a co-educational secondary school is putting herself in a position of high visibility. She knows she will have to prove herself to sceptics, and may also have to endure adverse sexist comment – hazards which male applicants do not have to consider. Less-successful men can be hostile to successful women (Cunnison, 1989).

In their interview study of highly successful women, Gerver and Hart spoke to a female educationist whose experience had shown her how 'very often men are either suspicious of women or contemptuous of them. Many men find it difficult to relate to a female boss' (Gerver and Hart, 1991, p. 111). Women heads may find themselves isolated from their male peers and may not have the benefit of easy networking for guidance and support (Marshall, 1985). Even other women heads may be less than wholly sympathetic, since successful women sometimes fail to see the difficulties that women generally labour under (Powney and Weiner, 1992). One reason is suggested by a senior business woman: 'Prejudice is so deeply ingrained that people don't even notice it ... It's hard to be heard, hard to be taken seriously by men' (Grassick, 1993, p. 23). There are obvious reasons why it may be difficult for the successful to see the system as just. One of Gerver and Hart's interviewees describes women as 'their own worst enemies' (p. 85) and the same study showed there was only minimal unqualified support for the women's movement among highly successful women (p. 160).

Another phenomenon which contributes to deterring any but the most ambitious is the new dominance of a managerial-ist philosophy in schools. A tight management structure is presented as the solution to many educational ills – although these perceived ills too often tend to be organizational and institutional, rather than the human problems of children's learning failing to develop. This philosophy is sometimes seen as devised by men in their own image, perhaps because it appears to be derived from the world of business with its deeply entrenched male ascendancy. 'Management' suggests designing and implementing procedures which will solve problems logically and systematically. It is associated with concepts like 'efficiency' and 'end-product' rather than with 'nurturing' or 'the development of the child'. This image of what is desirable in schools is strengthened by a political climate which claims that schools have long been ailing and failing, and that what they require is an injection of sound business methods in which top–down line management is seen as central. Clearly this idea appeals to politicians, since, in principle, it allows policies to be sent down the line to classroom teachers whose autonomy is thereby further diminished.

There is evidence that the new managerialism may be uncongenial to women in so far as women who do reach the upper echelons of secondary schooling tend to reject this style of leadership in favour of a style which is more democratic, collaborative, consultative, and participative (Powney and Weiner, 1992; Burton, 1993). In fact, despite popular views to the contrary, much of this type of approach is now used in modern industries which, for example, try to avoid confrontational disputes between management and work-force. It may therefore be that the leadership styles adopted by women in senior management positions are particularly effective. Alternatively, it may simply be that to become a secondary head in the first place, a women has to be outstandingly able.

Interestingly, where the worth of potential women leaders *is* recognized is not so much on the interview circuit as in the schools where they are already working. Hill (1994), in his study of primary headteachers in England, noted a tendency for women to have won these posts from the position of an internal candidate. Interviews with the few female secondary heads in Scotland suggest a similar phenomenon. Perhaps because women applicants fail to fit the norm, selectors see

73

the appointment of a woman to a headship as an exceptional choice; but where a woman's work and ability are already known to those with the power to make the appointment, the 'risk' factor is absent and such a woman has a fair chance of getting the post.

Part of the problem seems to be that the visible predominance of men in top posts in education exerts an invisible force on our collective mental set to the point where it becomes hard for many in our society to see that things could or should be otherwise. The position of secondary headteacher – a position of authority – is powerfully affected by a mental set produced by a long, and little varying, tradition of male appointments. In the mid-1970s one commentator observed: 'The school is traditionally seen by many adults as a restraining influence; the principal should be a deterrent figure, a remote authority to stop youth from running berserk' (Nisbet, 1975, p. 11). There was, and still is, a strong public expectation that a headteacher will act, not just as an educational leader, but also as an authority figure who is ultimately responsible for the effective control of young people's behaviour. In the days, not long gone, of corporal punishment, the 'strong arm' of the male head was not just a metaphor. The authority figure was necessarily seen as a male.

The legal prohibition of discrimination has been a useful counter to such ideas, but it is no substitute for changing the preconceptions of those in power. Rosemary Grant highlights a revealing impression from a woman who was interviewed for a headship:

> The tenor of the interview seemed to suggest that the ideal person for this job would be a man of a certain age, certain male attributes. Do you think you could live up to this? Would you find it difficult to take assemblies? How would you deal with a fight? I suspect they would have assumed that any man can deal with a fight in the playground. (Grant, 1989, p. 46)

In similar vein, a woman in a senior post in Scottish education claims: 'Like goes for like. Job descriptions are very often drawn up with a particular person – who just happens to be male – in mind' (Gerver and Hart, 1991, p. 84).

Public preconceptions, and particularly the preconceptions of the powerful, are surely the crux of the problem. Women may assume many more of the everyday responsibilities for childcare than do men in our society. Women are certainly more likely to experience breaks in employment. But these points can surely be seen as positive indicators of a more balanced outlook on life, rather than as isolating experiences which marginalize women's careers. Customarily, however, they have led to a widespread conviction that men are more 'dedicated' to their work, with all that can follow from such a view. Etzioni's book, for example, goes on to argue that: 'Their [women's] lesser career commitment may make them less creative in the long-range planning needed in upper-echelon positions' (Simpson and Simpson, 1969, p. 230). The evidence for such a claim is non-existent. On the contrary, the evidence we have presented in this chapter clearly shows that women teachers still do not get their fair share of promoted posts.

5 Pupils and outcomes

In this chapter we begin to look at differences in pupils' experiences at school, and in particular at differences between boys and girls in terms of educational outcomes towards the end of the schooling process. However, although the importance of performance indicators, such as examination results and the first destinations of pupils on leaving school, is growing in the eyes of parents and of politicians, it must nevertheless be recognized that there is more to education than this. Young people in our society spend 15,000 hours in classrooms, and only in the second half of this process of schooling do they even begin to look ahead to Standard grades, or to their equivalent GCSEs. If we can use examination results to tell something about an end-product, is there any comparable way of assessing the process which leads up to this point?

Among the research community, the measurement of interaction between pupils and teachers has been a popular way of indicating the nature of pupils' classroom experiences, with numerous studies counting up the number of occasions and different ways in which teachers interact with girls in the class, and comparing this with the number of interactions with boys. These various kinds of teacher–pupil interactions are generally classified under such headings as instructing, questioning, praising, and criticizing.

Investigations of this type have been collated and analysed by Alison Kelly (1988) who confirmed that these studies consistently show girls receiving less attention than boys. As was indicated by one of the earliest investigations to adopt this approach (Brophy and Good, 1970) the only measurable form of interaction where girls scored higher than boys was the frequency with which they offered to answer a question. Their offers of answers, however, were taken up by the teacher less often than with male volunteers. At one level, this may seem an insignificant finding, yet it suggests a number of potentially important points. Girls would appear to be more diligent and conscientious, and girls attempt to participate and involve themselves, whilst teachers tend not to respond fully to these attempts. Kelly found that:

> ... girls were particularly under-involved in lessons on science and social studies. In mathematics the overall participation of girls was as great as in other subjects, but they were markedly under-represented in instructional contacts. (Kelly, 1988, p. 8)

According to Kelly, measures of praise and criticism show male teachers paying less attention to female pupils, although measures of teaching showed girls getting lower levels of attention from women teachers also (i.e. less than their fair share) (p. 13). A recent study by Merrett and Wheldall (1992) distinguished between primary and secondary schooling. At the primary stage, no significant difference in levels of praise and criticism was found between girls and boys, or between male and female teachers. In secondary school, however, boys were given both more praise and more criticism. Women teachers were particularly likely to give more criticism to boys for misbehaviour than to girls, while men teachers tended to give more praise to boys for their schoolwork.

This kind of research invites a range of critical responses. First of all, it may be said that the overall order of difference in the attention given by teachers to girls and boys (44 per cent : 56 per cent) is not great. Kelly counter-argues that if this apparently modest discrepancy is quantified in terms of hours over an extended period of time, the first four years of secondary school, for example, the relative neglect of girls is substantial. And, importantly, MacIntosh (1990) found that girls were *aware* that teachers paid more attention to boys; so the real significance of the disparity may be that both girls and boys are encouraged to regard boys and their activities as more worthy of attention. However, it could be pointed out that making up part of the 'attention shortfall' is the relative lack of criticism which is focused on girls' academic performance, or (and here the discrepancy is more pronounced) on their behaviour. Parsons *et al.* (1982) argue, with regard to academic performance, that where an identifiable group has its work criticized more often (i.e. boys) the message is conveyed that a higher standard of achievement is expected. This may be so, but the fact that behavioural criticism is primarily directed at boys cannot reasonably be construed as conveying a positive message to boys, or a negative one to girls, although such criticisms may well simply serve to reinforce pupils' perceptions of what represents appropriate and acceptable 'male' and 'female' behaviour.

A recent large-scale study of young people in Scotland (Hendry *et al.*, 1993) has shown that girls have more favourable attitudes to school, and that they are less likely to react against the pressures to conform. The tendency to overt displays of rebelliousness on the part of boys, which is arguably part of a particular form of male sub-culture in secondary schools, clearly has the potential to inhibit academic success. Teachers may therefore consider it to be right to see boys as requiring more attention, and to see boys as requiring active encouragement to apply themselves. Passive acceptance or sullen rejection on the part of girls, however, are hardly more conducive to learning. Further, Riddell (1992) notes that there now exists a literature on female sub-cultures, which suggests that there may be a significant and emergent sub-group of girls who are also disaffected and highly rejecting of secondary school. This contrasts with the relatively passive and subordinate role often reported as typical of girls' experiences (Stanworth, 1981). Delamont (1984) has highlighted the important impact of sex roles and sex-role inequalities in schools. These, allied to relatively positive attitudes towards school and education, may represent a dilemma for some young women: that of combining a subordinate and passive role with academic success.

In the context of the present discussion, however, many researchers and teachers alike tend to portray boys as presenting a problem, while girls do not. Alternatively, and often concurrently, girls are also seen to present a problem, with passivity (and other female deficiencies) offered as explanations for lower levels of interaction. As we have noted, this may be too simple; there appears to be a danger in all this of representing boys and girls as two homogeneous groups. In one very detailed study, for example, French and French (1984) found that it was not boys in general who demanded more attention, but identifiable sub-groups of boys. The suggestion here is that the statistical imbalance between the attention paid to boys and the attention paid to girls is explicable in terms of particular boys, rather than boys as a group. A similar point could, of course, be made about the findings for girls.

But what are the longer-term impacts of pupils' responses to the schooling process, as reflected by inequalities in teacher–pupil interactions, and by the active rejection of the dominant values of secondary school among some boys (and to a lesser extent girls)? Do such factors affect outcomes for boys and girls, and in what ways? We begin to address these questions by exploring the present pattern of gender differences in performance in national examinations in Scotland in the later stages of secondary education: Standard grade examinations at 15–16 years of age (at the end of a fourth year of statutory secondary schooling) and Higher grade at 16–17 years of age (at the end of an optional fifth year).*

Table 5.1 provides an overall picture of gender differences in performance on the Standard grade by fourth year school

---

* Pupils are officially eligible to leave school in Scotland once they have reached their sixteenth birthday, at the end of the fourth year, or after one term of a fifth year (Christmas leavers) in the case of those pupils who are not yet sixteen by the official leaving date.

Table 5.1: Level of award on the Standard grade by gender (fourth year school candidates). Scotland, 1992.
Source: SEB, 1993.

| | Level of Award at Standard Grade | | | | |
	Credit	General	Foundation	Grade 7[a]	All Presentations
Female	56%	50%	43%	40%	50%
Male	44%	50%	57%	60%	50%
All	32%	49%	18%	1%	100%

[a] course completed but did not pass examination

candidates. Pupils typically present for examination in a range of Standard grade subjects, with all pupils expected to attempt Standard grade mathematics and English. The intention is to operate an educational and examination system which allows for assessment and certification of all fourth year pupils on Standard grade. At the present time, most fourth year pupils are presented for assessment in between 6 and 8 Standard grade subjects, with girls attempting slightly more Standard grades on average than boys (7.8 compared to 7.4 in 1994). Awards in each subject on the Standard grade range from grades 1 to 7, with an additional 'ungraded' category for those pupils who fail to complete the necessary course work. These grades also denote three levels of award: credit (the two highest grades 1 and 2), general (grades 3 and 4), and foundation (grades 5 and 6). Grade 7 denotes a completed course of study but failure to pass the exam. As can be seen from Table 5.1 (results for 1992), although there are roughly equal numbers of presentations by fourth year male and female pupils, overall, girls clearly do better than boys. Girls were more likely than boys to attain grades 1 and 2 at the highest (credit) level (56 per cent : 44 per cent) and they were correspondingly less likely to be graded at foundation level (43 per cent : 57 per cent). A very similar picture is evident from comparable GCSE results for the academic year 1992–3 in England (DFE, 1994a) with girls clearly doing better than boys. And the most recent Scottish data for 1994 shows that girls continue to do better at Standard grade.

Why is it that in terms of final outcomes of four years of secondary school education, boys do less well than girls in national examinations, where these examinations are specifically intended as a means of assessment and certification for all pupils? Some boys may simply be less 'able' than their peers in a number of ways. Putting aside biological explanations as a *direct* cause, and looking at the internalization of *responses* to biological difference (i.e. the socialization of learned gender 'appropriate' roles) it may be that boys are less able to conform to the expectations of the secondary school system, for example, and consequently more likely to reject the dominant values of such a system. The findings of French and French (1984) and those of Hendry *et al.* (1993) certainly suggest that it is a sub-group of males who are highly negative and rejecting of school. It may therefore be that a significant number of males (and a small number of females) see little value in secondary school, and so perceive early entry into the labour market as a more pressing concern, with the attendant 'adult status' associated with employment and wages. To some extent, these views may represent an accurate picture of the segmentation of the youth labour market by gender. In the case of young women at this age, girls tend to be more positive about school, to see greater value in education, and to stay on at school longer than boys. More, however, may in fact mean less for some young women (Dex, 1987) who may be disappointed in their expectations. It is important to recognize that staying on at school in order to attain more and better qualifications than their male contemporaries, does not necessarily result in improved labour market opportunities for young women. An extra year at school may still result in a 'lower' status occupation in the longer run.

Moving on one year in the process, Table 5.2 provides an overall picture of performance by fifth year school candidates

81

Table 5.2: Band of award on the Higher grade by gender (fifth year school candidates). Scotland, 1992.
Source: SEB, 1993.

| | Band of Award at Higher Grade | | | | |
	Band A	Band B	Band C	Band D	All Presentations
Female	52%	54%	54%	53%	53%
Male	48%	46%	46%	47%	47%
All	18%	27%	33%	22%	100%

on the Higher grade (results for 1992). Bands A–C represent a pass at Higher grade, with band A the highest level of award. Scottish Highers are taken one year earlier than English A levels, with some pupils sitting a second diet of Higher examinations in their sixth year. First, it is notable that there are significantly fewer presentations by males (47 per cent : 53 per cent). This is principally because a greater proportion of males leave school early, at the end of the compulsory period of secondary education, without attempting an optional fifth year of study. However, what is most notable from these data is that the picture changes between the fourth and fifth years. From a position where girls clearly do better in fourth year examinations, the aggregate picture provided by Table 5.2 shows very little evidence of gender differences one year later. The most recent set of Higher results for fifth year candidates in 1994 confirms this general picture, with some slight indications that girls do better than boys overall at Higher grade.

A very plausible explanation for this changing in gender differences in achievement between fourth and fifth years of school would be that a sub-group of less 'able', poorly 'motivated' or disaffected male pupils leave school early, and so do not present at Higher grade. Alternatively, it may also be that the Higher grade curriculum is more 'conventional' and that this makes Highers more suited than Standard grades to male pupils. From 1986 Standard grades began to replace the previous Ordinary grade examinations in Scottish schools, and by 1992 had superseded them. These changes in the arrangements for certification and assessment of fourth year pupils, which have resulted in the present Standard grade curriculum, may help to explain the better performance of girls. Research (SEB, 1995) suggests that gender differences in Standard grade examination results for 1993 are related to variations in performance within the various elements which go to make up the assessment of each subject. In general, the differences in favour of girls within particular Standard grade subjects tend to be greatest in the element of Investigating, as opposed to elements such as Knowledge and Understanding. Girls, for example, tend to do better than boys overall in project-based investigations.

Examination results for 17-year-olds at A/AS level in England in the year 1992–3 show that males overall did better than females (DFE, 1994a) in that year. A higher proportion of young women took A/AS levels than young men, but male candidates tended to pass more subjects, and to get slightly higher grades than female candidates. A more detailed analysis of the A/AS level performance in 1992, which also takes account of the prior attainment of pupils at GCSE, shows that boys still did better than girls (DFE, 1994b). In other words, males did better than females at A/AS level, even when comparisons are made between pupils with similar levels of prior attainment at GCSE. Thus, in England, from a position of relative advantage in terms of GCSE results, at 15 years of age, girls did less well than boys two years later, at 17 years of age, and this phenomenon is not accounted for by a sub-group of less 'able' boys leaving secondary school early to become economically active. However, as has been brought to everyone's attention by the hysterical reaction of some elements of the media to more recent A/AS level examination results, the situation has since changed in England, and we are informed that 'women are now winning the education and employment race!' Our own conclusion would be that – in terms of national examination results – the pictures in Scotland and England are now broadly similar, with girls very clearly doing better than boys at Standard grade and at GCSE, whilst overall differences between girls and boys subsequently narrow and are less evident at Higher grade and at AS/A level.

From a slightly different perspective, we can also examine educational outcomes in terms of the qualifications held by all school leavers (from fourth, fifth, and sixth years taken together) in a particular academic year (1992–3), rather than comparing the performance of male and female pupils within the same year group (15- to 16-year-olds in fourth year, or 16- to 17-year olds in fifth year). In other words, we can look at the stock of educational resource available for use in the labour market or the tertiary education sector among all school leavers in any one year. We can also take a longer-term view, by looking at changing patterns over an eleven-year period, from 1982–3 to 1992–3. In Scotland, this period includes the shift from Ordinary grades to Standard grades as a means of certification (roughly equivalent to replacing O levels with GCSEs in England).

Table 5.3 presents details of the highest (Scottish Certificate of Education) qualification held by school leavers for the years 1982–3, 1987–8, and 1992–3. The introduction of the Standard grade has resulted in a decrease in the proportion of pupils leaving school with no qualifications, and a corresponding increase in the proportion leaving with qualifications lower than Standard grades 1–3 (or Ordinary grades A–C). (This is not surprising, given the aim of Standard grade was to ensure assessment for all.) The effect is compounded by a number of factors, however, including marked changes in staying on rates, perhaps as a result of a contracting youth labour market (Bynner, 1987). The proportions leaving with Standard grades at 1–3 have remained relatively constant over the eleven-year period, but most notably the percentage leaving with at least one Higher grade pass (bands A–C) has risen progressively from 33 per cent to 43 per cent. Thus, there was a general

Table 5.3: School leavers by gender and highest SCE qualification. Scotland, 1982–3, 1987–8, and 1992–3.

Source: SOED, 1994.

Academic year	Total leavers (= 100%)	Highest SCE qualification held							
			Standard grades				Higher grades at bands A–C		
			All grade	At Grade 1–3[b]					
		None	4–7[a]	1 or 2	3 or 4	5 +	1 or 2	3 or 4	5 +
Females									
1982–3	(44,226)	24%	9%	15%	10%	7%	14%	12%	10%
1987–8	(37,140)	13%	14%	16%	10%	8%	15%	13%	12%
1992–3	(28,262)	9%	13%	14%	9%	8%	16%	14%	17%
Males									
1982–3	(46,762)	28%	9%	16%	9%	8%	10%	9%	10%
1987–8	(38,919)	17%	16%	18%	9%	8%	12%	9%	11%
1992–3	(29,534)	12%	18%	16%	9%	8%	12%	11%	14%

[a] including O' grades D, E/4, 5
[b] including O' grades A to C/1 to 3

increase in the level of qualifications of Scottish school leavers from 1982–3 to 1992–3.

Turning to gender differences within this overall picture of change, girls continued to leave school with better qualifications than boys throughout the eleven-year period, although such differences were less marked at higher levels of attainment. However, from a position of equality in 1982–3, the percentage who left school with the very highest levels of attainment has increased more rapidly among girls than boys, with 17 per cent of girls as opposed to 14 per cent of boys leaving school with five or more Higher passes in 1992–3. Thus, throughout a period of considerable change within schools and society more generally, young women would appear to have maintained a position of relative advantage over their male counterparts in terms of the outcomes of secondary schooling (as gauged by exam performance) and if anything they have apparently improved their position at the highest levels of attainment. Once more, the conclusion is that girls tend to do better than boys at secondary school. A very similar picture of gender differences in school leavers' qualifications is also evident in England over the eleven-year period 1981–2 to 1991–2 (DOE, 1993a) where, for example, from a position of relative equality at the beginning of this period, the proportion of pupils leaving school with higher levels of qualifications has increased more rapidly among girls than boys.

Girls may well do better than boys at secondary school, and they leave school with more and better qualifications, but what of their immediate prospects post-school? We address this question by first building up a general picture of the destinations of one cohort (1989–90) of Scottish school leavers in the spring of the following year (1991) and we then examine in detail more recent data relating to one cohort of (local authority) school leavers in the Grampian region, in the north-east of Scotland. Although the local youth labour market situation in Grampian cannot be regarded as typical of the general situation in Scotland, or indeed Britain, the data presented for the region's secondary schools do serve to highlight some key differences in the labour market position of young men and women on leaving school.

Looking first at the picture for all Scottish leavers at the beginning of the 1990s, the data presented in Table 5.4 show that males were more likely than females to be economically active (i.e. in full-time employment or training) whilst females were more likely than males to continue in full-time education on leaving school, although raised levels of female participation in tertiary education were focused more within further education, rather than higher education.

Turning to a more recent and more detailed examination of the situation for school leavers in Grampian, young men are more likely than young women to leave the region's schools early, as can be seen from the final row of Table 5.5, and as the third and fourth rows of the same table show, males are also more likely than females to be economically active on leaving school, particularly amongst early leavers. Hence,

Table 5.4: First destinations of school leavers. Scotland, 1989–90.
Source: SOED, 1992.

Destination at Spring 1991	Female	Male
Leavers entering:		
Higher education	20%	18%
Non-advanced further education and other non-advanced courses	13%	9%
Full-time employment (not YT)	31%	34%
Youth training	21%	27%
Unemployed and other destinations	15%	13%
All leavers	49%	51%

Table 5.5: First destinations of those leaving local authority secondary schools. Grampian Region, September 1992.
Source: GRCED Careers Service, 1992.

First destination	Fourth year leavers		Fifth year leavers		Sixth year leavers	
	Female	Male	Female	Male	Female	Male
Leavers entering:						
Higher education	0%	0%	7%	7%	49%	53%
Further education	27%	12%	30%	21%	19%	13%
Full-time employment	45%	57%	40%	47%	17%	19%
Training	7%	11%	5%	8%	1%	1%
Unemployed and other destinations	17%	16%	14%	13%	11%	11%
Unavailable	4%	4%	4%	3%	3%	3%
All leavers	41%	59%	54%	46%	56%	44%

males are more likely than females to leave school early and to enter employment or training. By contrast, early a female leavers are much more likely than males to enter a further education college. Amongst those pupils who stay on at school for an additional fifth and sixth years in Grampian, males are marginally more likely than females to enter higher education on leaving school. These findings correspond quite closely to the overall pattern of gender differences noted at the national level, with the exception of entry to higher education. There is also some evidence of higher rates of entry to full-time employment (as opposed to employment training) amongst both male and female leavers in Grampian, when comparisons are made with the situation in Scotland overall. Thus, to summarize these findings for first destinations of school leavers, it would appear that a greater proportion of male compared to female leavers enter full-time employment or training on leaving school, whereas a greater proportion of female compared to male leavers enter full-time education; but this over-representation of women entrants to the post-school education sector is principally focused on non-advanced courses in further education colleges. If we exclude those school leavers who enter higher education (typically after six years of secondary schooling) then we have a picture of male leavers as rejecting full-time education, allied to a disposition to enter employment or training. Whether female leavers are more positive about full-time further education, or whether the types of employment and training opportunities which are available to young women leave them with fewer choices (except to stay on at school, or to go to college) is another question.

Whatever the answer to the question of what represents the better opportunities in the longer term – employment and training, or further education college – it is very clear from the additional data presented in Table 5.6 that employment within the youth labour market in the Grampian region (and elsewhere in Scotland) is strongly segmented along gender lines. Here, the types of employment entered by young women on leaving school are concentrated within the service sectors (e.g. caring, retail, clerical, secretarial, and catering) whilst the jobs of male leavers are concentrated within construction, engineering, factory, and outdoor work. This makes meaningful comparisons between the sexes problematic, and it also begs the question as to whether these first destinations reflect

Table 5.6: Categories of employment of those entering work on leaving local authority secondary schools. Grampian Region, September 1992. *Source*: GRCED Careers Service, 1992.

| | Categories of employment | | | | | | | | | |
	Caring/ security	Retail sales	Clerical/ secretarial	Catering	Factory work	Con- struction	Outdoor	Engin- eering	Other	All categories
Female	85%	74%	68%	62%	38%	28%	25%	8%	44%	45%
Males	15%	26%	32%	38%	62%	72%	75%	92%	56%	55%
All	9%	15%	15%	8%	11%	16%	5%	14%	7%	100%

the opportunities available, or whether they represent the occupational 'choices' that young people are qualified for and aspire to.

Do earlier 'choices' made by pupils at secondary school anticipate these gender differences in subsequent labour market position and types of employment? Pupils follow a common curriculum in first and second years of secondary school in Scotland, with choices for third and fourth year made during the spring of the second year. Third and fourth year pupils choose subjects within a nationally agreed curriculum framework (where subjects are grouped into modes) and pupils are expected to study Standard grades in English, mathematics, a scientific subject (biology, chemistry, physics, or general science), a social and environmental subject (history, modern studies, geography, etc.), a modern language (French, German, etc.), a technological activity (office and information studies, home economics, social and vocational skills, craft and design, etc.) and a creative and aesthetic activity (art, music, physical education, etc.). Short courses or modules also supplement the Standard grade curriculum for some pupils, but only within a very restricted range of choice. The aim is to ensure that all pupils study Standard grades from within a common curriculum framework.

Table 5.7 lists eighteen Standard grade subjects (these are the subjects with the largest numbers of candidates) and

Table 5.7: Presentations and level of award on the Standard grade by gender (fourth year school candidates and for subjects representing more than 2% of total presentations by fourth year candidates). Scotland, 1992.
Source: SEB, 1993.

S' Grade subject	Level of award				S' Grade subject	Level of award			
	Credit	General	Founda-tion	All presenta-tions		Credit	General	Founda-tion	All presenta-tions
*Office and information studies***					*English****				
Female	89%	83%	74%	84%	Female	60%	47%	28%	50%
Male	11%	17%	26%	16%	Male	40%	53%	72%	50%
*Home economics****					*Mathematics*NS				
Female	96%	86%	63%	78%	Female	48%	50%	49%	49%
Male	4%	14%	37%	22%	Male	52%	50%	51%	51%
*Biology****					*Chemistry*NS				
Female	72%	71%	66%	70%	Female	48%	48%	49%	48%
Male	28%	29%	34%	30%	Male	52%	52%	51%	52%
*Music****					*Science****				
Female	68%	63%	44%	63%	Female	44%	41%	45%	44%
Male	32%	37%	56%	37%	Male	56%	59%	55%	56%
*French****					*Geography****				
Female	65%	56%	44%	57%	Female	48%	40%	36%	42%
Male	35%	44%	56%	43%	Male	52%	60%	64%	58%
*Modern studies****					*Computing***				
Female	63%	56%	49%	56%	Female	37%	37%	33%	36%
Male	37%	44%	51%	44%	Male	63%	63%	67%	64%
*History****					*Physical education****				
Female	63%	58%	45%	56%	Female	28%	33%	42%	32%
Male	37%	42%	55%	44%	Male	72%	67%	58%	68%
*Art****					*Physics****				
Female	66%	52%	34%	54%	Female	34%	27%	26%	31%
Male	34%	48%	66%	46%	Male	66%	73%	74%	69%
*Social and vocational studies****					*Craft and design****				
Female	70%	50%	37%	52%	Female	20%	14%	12%	15%
Male	30%	50%	63%	48%	Male	80%	86%	88%	85%

NS not significant, * P < 0.01, ** P < 0.001, *** P < 0.0001 provides details of presentations and attainment for Scotland in 1992. The Standard grade subjects in the table are ordered in terms of the proportions of female to male candidates, running from predominantly 'female' subjects (top right of the table) through to predominantly 'male' subjects (bottom left of the table). Standard grade subjects where there is a marked over-representation of girls (more than 60 per cent of candidates) include: office and information studies, home economics, biology, and music. Standard grade subjects where there is a marked under-representation of girls (less than 40 per cent of candidates) include: computing studies, physical education, physics, and craft and design. All pupils are expected to study mathematics and English, which explains their central position in the table. As was noted above, there are other constraints on subject choice within the Standard grade curriculum, for example, the requirement that at least one scientific subject is studied. Nevertheless, with a few exceptions (which would appear to be as a direct result of such curricular constraints) the patterning of subject 'choice' by gender is often reminiscent of prescriptions on the suitability of subjects for young men and women from the Edwardian era, rather than the present time. Thus, at the extremes of choice: young women study life sciences, concern themselves with the home and office, and develop an appreciation of music; whilst young men study physical sciences, concern themselves with the workshop and computer, and develop the physical self.

It is true to say, however, that there have been some significant changes in patterns of choice over the last twenty years. Croxford (1994) has shown that since the introduction of the Sex Discrimination Act (1975) and the implementation of (and amendments to) a common curriculum framework in local authority schools (SED, 1983, 1989) there has been an equalization in the representation of girls and boys within the various modes of the curriculum (e.g. English and modern languages, mathematical studies, scientific studies, social and environmental studies, technological activities, and aesthetic and creative activities). This has been particularly notable within the scientific mode, for example, where the picture has altered dramatically. From a point in the mid- 1970s where fewer than one-half of girls studied a science, all girls are now expected to do so. The increase amongst boys has been from around two-thirds to almost all. Nevertheless, Croxford notes that large differences are still to be found for individual subjects within modes, for example, biology and physics within the scientific mode.

A report by HM Inspectors of schools, which was published twenty years ago (HMI, 1975) further highlights the significant changes that have occurred in recent years, and the changes that were already taking place in the period immediately prior to the era of the Sex Discrimination Act. The report compares the 'opportunities for educational development open to boys and girls in Scottish secondary schools' and concludes that with respect to subject choice:

> Curricular patterns are not static: the nature of subject choice, as exercised by boys and girls, shows substantial change even over a brief time span. [Here, comparisons were made between the years 1967 and 1972.] Movement is marked in the case of academic subjects, significantly less so in the case of subjects which are more ostensibly technical and vocational. (HMI, 1975, p. 39)

Nevertheless, based on a survey of thirty-two secondary schools, the report notes that in 1974 there were still marked differences in patterns of subject choice amongst third and fourth year pupils. Overall, for example, there were low percentages of boys in home economics and business studies (both around 15 per cent) and very low percentages of girls in technical subjects (around 2 per cent). If we now look at the picture some eighteen years later (see Table 5.7) the percentages of boys in office and information studies (16 per cent) and in home economics (22 per cent) are not that different from those reported in 1974, and although there is clear evidence of change in technological subjects (e.g. the percentage of female presentations in craft and design was 15 per cent in 1992) girls remain very much in the minority in such subjects. Also, if Ordinary grade subjects are labelled in terms of the proportions of girls to boys presenting for examination in 1973, then running through the curriculum from predominantly 'female' subjects to predominantly 'male' subjects, we have: secretarial studies, home economics, biology, music, French, history, modern studies, art, English, mathematics, chemistry, geography, physics, building drawing, and engineering drawing. If we do the same for comparable Standard grade subjects in 1992, we have: office and information studies, home economics, biology, music, French, modern studies, history, art, English, mathematics, chemistry, geography, physics, craft and design. A dramatic about-turn in patterns of choice by gender across the curriculum, with modern studies and history exchanging positions! There have certainly been some important changes in the *opportunities* open to girls and boys in Scottish secondary schools over the past twenty years, but how much *actual change* has actually occurred?

Thus, a clear pattern of gender differences persists within the curriculum at the present time. And yet, girls still do significantly better than boys, not only overall, but in fourteen out of the eighteen subjects listed in Table 5.7, including subjects at the 'male' end of the curriculum, such as physics, and craft and design. In two subjects only do boys attain better grades than girls at Standard grade: to some extent in general science, and markedly so in physical education. A closer examination of physical education reveals that the better performance of boys is largely restricted to the practical element of the subject (SEB, 1995). One might also ask why there is not a clearer pattern of differences in mathematics and chemistry, given the raised levels of attainment by girls elsewhere in the curriculum. However, it is perhaps more important to note that girls do better than boys in most Standard grade subjects, and with the exceptions of general science and physical education, they do as well as and often better than boys within predominantly 'male' areas of the curriculum, and within subjects which are regarded as (stereotypically) requiring distinctively 'male' attributes.

In the case of mathematics, for example, there persists a popular belief that boys naturally excel – a view which is often justified by reference to psychological research which supposedly demonstrates the greater innate ability of males in spatial and other skills. If the results of national examinations are not enough to dispel such popular misconceptions, the work of Baker and Jones (1992) offers further compelling evidence to challenge such 'common-sense' views. Utilizing cross-national data, Baker and Jones examined variations in (academic) mathematical ability among 13-year-old girls and boys in different countries, and concluded that *social* factors were central to explanations of gender differences in school mathematics attainment at this age. They argued that performance was linked to pupils' perceptions of future opportunities, with current achievement seen as some sort of currency or resource to be spent in the future in order to gain access to further educational or occupational opportunities.

Whether this argument is valid or not, the findings reported by Baker and Jones are nevertheless of considerable importance, in that they highlight some key points about gender differences and academic performance. First, differences in performance were not invariant across countries: in some places boys did better than girls, in others there were few differences, whilst in others girls did better than boys. The size and direction of such gender differences in attainment were dependent on the country. Second, differences between boys and girls were not invariant over time. Comparisons were made with the situation two decades earlier, and it was found that from a position where males did better in the great majority of countries, there was clear evidence of an overall reduction in differences over time, with a shift towards equalization or relative advantage for girls. Third, it was shown that the extent and direction of differences between girls and boys were linked to the educational and occupational status of adult women within the countries under consideration. In countries where more opportunities were available for adult women, girls' performances were also better. So girls perceptions of their future opportunities in our society (and others) not only influence the 'choices' that girls make at school, but such perceptions may also affect how well girls' perform at school. And central to young women's perceptions of their future roles must be the messages conveyed by that society, where these are promoted, reinforced, or challenged by the process of schooling.

6 Patterns of subject choice: a local study

In this chapter we continue our exploration of pupils' experiences in secondary school by examining a number of aspects of subject choice and career intention in more depth. This is done by shifting the focus away from a broad-based statistical picture at the national level, and towards a more localized picture which is based on the results of an on-going study of pupils in education authority comprehensive schools in one region of Scotland. The Grampian Equal Opportunities (Grampian EO) study is centred on seven of the region's secondary schools. These schools were purposely chosen to represent a variety of settings within what is a geographically diverse area, covering most of the north-east of Scotland around the one major city in the region, Aberdeen.

Three of the schools participating in the study are situated in Aberdeen. One is located in a part of the city which comprises predominantly rented council housing, and where there are some significant pockets of urban deprivation. Another of the urban schools serves a more mixed catchment, but still has a high proportion of council housing, although the majority are now owner-occupied. The third city school is situated in a more affluent suburban area of new housing, with parental occupations spread widely across the skilled manual and service classes. The most 'middle class' of the seven schools, however, is set in a more rural context. This fourth school is located within commuting distance of Aberdeen, and there has been much in-migration in recent years, due largely to the growth of an oil economy in the region. A further two of the study's schools have smaller rolls and are highly rural in character, being over 50 kilometres from the urban centre in Aberdeen. The final school is a typical large burgh comprehensive, situated in a coastal town to the north of Aberdeen, where the traditional industries are a mix of fisheries and agriculture.

Thus, the schools represent seven distinct contexts, which cover most types of local authority secondary to be found in the region. The study was initiated through a process of negotiation and collaboration with each school, and the aim was to look at each context in depth, from the pupil, parent, and staff perspectives. It is notable that the research has been sponsored by, and has received much of its impetus from, TVEI (Technical and Vocational Education Initiative) in the region. One of the aims of TVEI is to address equality of opportunity, and access. As has been recently noted by the Equal Opportunities Commission, however, the impetus which gender issues has received from such initiatives may be under threat, due to the considerable and rapid change in arrangements for the management of local authority schools (with the break-up of education authorities, and opting-out, for example) and the unknown impact of curriculum reform (in the shape of the 5–14 curriculum in Scotland, or the National Curriculum in England).

In this chapter we utilize findings from one component of the Grampian study: a questionnaire survey of third and fourth year pupils in the seven secondary schools. The questionnaire was completed by 483 pupils under the guidance of a fieldworker at the beginning of the academic year in October 1994. The survey sample consisted of between 15 and 20 girls, and a similar number of boys, from each year group in each of the seven schools. In total, 120 third-year girls, 124 third-year boys, 116 fourth-year girls, and 123 fourth-year boys completed a questionnaire. Thus, the survey provides a profile of the self-perceptions of pupils from two year goups: one group had just entered fourth year (having made subject choices in the academic year 1991–2) and the other group had just entered third year (having made subject

97

choices in the academic year 1992–3). In what follows, our findings are based on data which are aggregated across the seven study schools. It may be that the sample of pupils obtained in this way is not representative of the school population in Grampian, nor indeed of Scotland, and certainly not of Britain. Although it is important to keep this in mind, the survey nevertheless allows us to explore differences between the choices and perceptions of girls and boys in some detail.

The data presented in Table 6.1 indicate the most commonly mentioned career choices of young people in the sample. These careers were the first choices of pupils, and were made in response to open-ended questions regarding future career intentions. Pupils' self-reports of career choices are clearly patterned by gender, with occupations in technological areas (e.g. engineering and craft and design) seen to be a predominantly male preserve, and occupations in caring (e.g. nursing and childcare) and junior non-manual positions (e.g. secretarial and clerical) seen to be predominantly female preserves. What is perhaps most striking, however, is the way in which the career aspirations of pupils from working-class (manual) home backgrounds are patterned by gender, with girls in this group much more likely to identify nursing, secretarial and clerical jobs, hairdressing, and childcare as intended careers, whereas boys are much more likely to identify trades in skilled manual occupations (e.g. builder, mechanic, joiner, electrician) as future jobs. Such differences are also evident to a lesser extent among young people from middle-class (non-manual) households (e.g. engineering for boys and teaching for girls).

The differences in the career intentions of working-class girls and boys in the sample to some extent reflect the types of employment entered by (early) school leavers in the Grampian region in recent years (see Table 5.6) although little mention is made of 'lower status' jobs in the retail and sales sector (females) or of factory work (males). Thus, young people's intended career choices are often highly stereotypical at this age, not only in terms of gender, but also in terms of gender within social class. Career aspirations are therefore already

Table 6.1:Intended career (first choice) by gender and social class of home back
ground (third and fourth year pupils in seven local authority secondary
schools).
Source: Grampian EO survey, 1994.

Career choice	Female non-manual household	Female manual household	Male non-manual household	Male manual household	Total (n = 100%)
Engineering	17%	0%	48%	35%	(n = 23)
Teaching	38%	27%	7%	27%	(n = 29)
Accountancy	39%	12%	39%	12%	(n = 16)
Architect, town planning	9%	9%	46%	36%	(n = 11)
Ship and aircraft officers	18%	0%	54%	27%	(n = 11)
Performing arts and sport	33%	20%	13%	33%	(n = 15)
Draughtsperson	6%	19%	50%	25%	(n = 21)
Nursing	31%	61%	8%	0%	(n = 13)
Secretarial and clerical	17%	71%	8%	4%	(n = 24)
Builder	0%	0%	9%	91%	(n = 11)
Mechanic	7%	0%	7%	86%	(n = 14)
Joiner, carpenter	0%	0%	0%	100%	(n = 19)
Chef, catering	13%	27%	13%	47%	(n = 15)
Hairdressing, beautician	36%	64%	0%	0%	(n = 11)
Childcare (nursery nurse)	35%	65%	0%	0%	(n = 17)
Police	18%	29%	24%	29%	(n = 17)
Armed forces	0%	20%	30%	50%	(n = 10)

[a] derived from an open-ended question, and for occupations mentioned by ten
or more pupils

divided along gender lines, well before young people leave
school.

The data presented in Table 6.2, however, emphasize that
this is an on-going process, with significant changes occurring
between third and fourth year of secondary school. Pupils are
asked to make subject choices mid-way through their second
year (which are assumed relevant to their educational and
occupational intentions) but it is clear from Table 6.2 that
some young people subsequently revise their plans for the
future. The table shows that the intention to continue in full-
time education or to enter the youth labour market on leaving
school is patterned by both gender and social class. This is

Table 6.2: Intended first destination on leaving school by gender and social class of home background (third and fourth year pupils in seven local authority secondary schools).
Source: Grampian EO survey, 1994.

First destination	Female non-manual household	Female manual household	Male non-manual household	Male manual household	All pupils
Third year pupils					
Enter employment/ training	40%	61%	50%	59%	55%
Continue full-time education	53%	33%	43%	32%	39%
Undecided	7%	6%	7%	8%	6%
Fourth year pupils					
Enter employment / training	19%	42%	41%	61%	43%
Continue full-time education	77%	51%	51%	31%	50%
Undecided	6%	7%	8%	8%	7%
All pupils	20%	29%	21%	30%	100%

important, since present policy is to raise staying-on rates in schools, and to encourage continuing education. Our data suggest that the intention to enter tertiary education (further or higher) on leaving school is related to both gender and class in a complex way. Girls from middle-class homes are most certain about continuing in full-time education, whilst males from working-class homes are least likely to see this as an option. The picture for working-class males remains unchanged between third and fourth year, but for all other groups there is a shifting focus away from early labour market entry towards continuing education, with this changing emphasis most marked among young women. Such findings are consistent with raised levels of entry to non-advanced further education courses among (early) female leavers in Grampian (see Table 5.5). It is particularly interesting to note that from a position at the start of the third year where around two-thirds of working-class girls see early employment as an imperative, only a minority do so by the beginning of the fourth year. Hence, among pupils from manual home backgrounds, at the start of the third year, equal numbers of boys and girls see early employment as likely. By the start of the fourth year, however, working-class boys continue to see this as the main aim, whereas working-class girls shift focus towards continuing education. These findings, as was argued in the previous chapter, indicate that a significant sub-group of boys (and to a lesser extent girls) may see little relevance in continuing education (secondary or tertiary) and the findings further show that the majority of these pupils come from working-class home backgrounds. A careful check on the data for each school (separately) confirms that the intention to enter employment immediately on leaving school is most marked among boys from manual home backgrounds: the effect is not confined to only one or two schools in the sample.

One of the aims of the Grampian EO study was to identify *patterns* of subject choice across the curriculum among third- and fourth-year pupils, rather than simply to look at gender differences within specific subjects. As we have already shown in the previous chapter (see Table 5.7) there are significant gender differences in attainment at Standard grade, largely in favour of girls, but it is with respect to subject uptake that differences between girls and boys are most marked. But what patterns of choice exist in secondary schools? In order to address this question, and not only with regard to gender differences, we conducted a cluster analysis of the subject choices made by our sample of third- and fourth-year pupils. The aim of the analysis was to see if it was possible to identify distinctive groupings of pupils, by examining patterns of subject choice across the third- and fourth-year curricula. Each of the subjects used to differentiate between pupils represented a genuine choice within all seven of the study schools. This meant that mathematics and English were excluded from the analysis as all pupils take these subjects. Further, when interpreting the patterns of choice made by pupils, it is important to bear in mind that the schools in the study offer a wide range of Standard grades from which to choose, but that these options are constrained both by a nationally agreed curriculum framework, and by the resources of the school. Since 1992, for example, all pupils in Scottish local authority secondary schools have been expected to take a Standard grade in a modern foreign language (e.g. French, German, Spanish or Italian) but in a smaller school this may mean that all pupils are expected to study the same modern language (normally French). Amongst a number of other constraints on choice, there is also a requirement that pupils study a Standard grade in at least one scientific subject (physics, chemistry, biology, or general science), and in a social sciences subject (geography, history, modern studies, or contemporary social studies). So what groupings of pupils can be identified from this interplay of choice and constraints?

Three distinct groups of pupil were extracted by the cluster analysis (see Table 6.3). The first and second groups (groups A and B) are of roughly equal size and together make up 60 per cent of the sample, whilst the third group (group C) is slightly larger and accounts for 37 per cent of pupils. (A further 3 per cent of pupils remain unclassified by the analysis.) Table 6.3 shows how the groups can be distinguished from each other in terms of the Standard grade subjects which pupils in each group are more (or less) likely to study. The major (most marked) difference between the three groups is with respect to choice of science subjects. In group A, 96 per cent of pupils take physics, 4 per cent take biology, 42 per cent take chemistry, and none take general science. In group B, 5 per cent of pupils take physics, 89 per cent take biology, 40 per cent take chemistry, and none take general science. In group C, 4 per cent of pupils take physics, 5 per cent take biology, 9 per cent take chemistry, and 82 per cent take general science. Thus, the great majority of pupils in group C study general science alone, whilst pupils in group A study physics (at the expense of biology and general science) and pupils in group B study biology (at the expense of physics and

Table 6.3: Patterns of subject choice of third and fourth year pupils in seven local authority secondary schools. Grampian Region, 1994. A typology (subject-choice groupings) of pupils in terms of Standard grade subjects, derived from a cluster analysis.
Source: Grampian EO survey, 1994.

Subject group	Differences among groups in terms of Standard grade subjects	
	More likely to study	Less likely to study
Group A (n = 139, 29%) μ - A	Physics Chemistry Geography Technological Studies Graphic Communication	Biology Science Modern Studies History Office and Information Studies Social and Vocational Studies Craft and Design Home Economics
Group B (n = 149, 31%) F - A	Biology Chemistry History Office and Information Studies Home Economics	Physics Science Geography Physical Education Craft and Design Technological Studies Graphic Communication
Group C (n = 178, 37%) N - A	Science Modern Studies or Social Studies Social and Vocational Studies Physical Education Craft and Design	Physics Biology Chemistry Geography History Art
Unclassified (n = 16, 3%)		

general science). There are further differences between the three groups, with pupils in group A favouring subjects where boys are over-represented (e.g. geography, technological studies, and graphic communication) and pupils in group B favouring subjects where girls are over-represented (e.g. history, office and information studies, and home

103

economics). These different patterns of subject choice would therefore suggest the following descriptive labels for pupils within the three groups: 'male-academic' orientation (group A), 'female-academic' orientation (group B), and 'non-academic' orientation (group C). One reason for labelling the third group of pupils as 'non-academic' in terms of subject choice would be that general science is offered as a means by which all pupils may study a scientific subject (i.e. as an alternative to physics, biology, or chemistry) but very few pupils are presented in general science at credit level (i.e. at the highest grades 1 and 2). The comments of a pupil from one of the study schools makes this clear:

> I wanted to do physics ... physics were turning folk away ... it was done on marks so I just took science. My sister was the same. She wanted to take biology, but she was told she wasn't smart enough to do it ... so she'd have to do like Standard grade science instead ... just take science.   (Fourth-year boy in urban comprehensive)

We now test the extent to which the labels we have used for the three subject-choice groupings of pupils may be justified. This is done by examining differences among the three groups with respect to other factors which were not included in the cluster analysis, particularly gender, social class background, and future occupational and educational intentions.

Table 6.4 shows that group membership is strongly linked to gender. Around three-quarters of the pupils in group A are boys, whilst three-quarters of the pupils in group B are girls. The numbers of girls and boys in group C are broadly similar, although there are marginally fewer girls than boys in this third group. Further, pupils in groups A and B are more likely to come from middle-class non-manual homes, whilst more than two-thirds of the pupils in group C come from manual home backgrounds (see Table 6.5).

Developing the profile of the three groups in terms of social class background more fully, the picture appears to be quite complex for young people in group B: boys in this group are more likely to come from middle-class homes, whereas girls in

Table 6.4: Patterns of subject choice by gender (third and fourth year pupils in seven local authority secondary schools).
Source: Grampian EO survey, 1994.

	Subject group			All pupils
	Group A	Group B	Group C	
Female	23%	76%	44%	49%
Male	77%	24%	56%	51%
All pupils	30%	32%	38%	100%

Table 6.5: Patterns of subject choice by gender and social class of home background (third and fourth year pupils in seven local authority secondary schools).
Source: Grampian EO survey, 1994.

Social class of head of household	Subject group			All pupils
	Group A	Group B	Group C	
Female				
Non-manual household	58%	38%	29%	38%
Manual household	39%	59%	64%	57%
Unclassified	3%	3%	7%	5%
Male				
Non-manual household	54%	51%	28%	38%
Manual household	42%	46%	65%	56%
Unclassified	4%	3%	7%	6%
All pupils	30%	32%	38%	100%

group B come from a mix of social backgrounds. One interpretation of these results would be that some girls from working-class homes are more likely than boys from similar backgrounds to consider continuing in full-time education (e.g. staying on at school, or going on to further education college) and so to choose Standard grades which reflect these aspirations (e.g. the more 'academic' biology, as opposed to general science, but certainly not physics).

Turning to measures of young people's future intentions and their relationship to the subject-choice groupings, around

Table 6.6: Patterns of subject choice by gender and intended career (third and fourth year pupils in seven local authority secondary schools). *Source:* Grampian EO Survey, 1994.

Social class of intended occupation	Subject group			All pupils
	Group A	Group B	Group C	
Female				
Professional	49%	34%	17%	30%
Skilled non-manual	36%	37%	38%	36%
Skilled manual	4%	5%	4%	4%
Semi/unskilled manual	11%	23%	41%	30%
Male				
Professional	42%	33%	16%	28%
Skilled non-manual	36%	38%	14%	26%
Skilled manual	15%	19%	53%	34%
Semi/unskilled manual	7%	10%	17%	12%
All pupils	30%	32%	38%	100%

three-quarters of pupils in groups A and B hope eventually to enter non-manual occupations, whereas many fewer pupils in group C expect to enter such occupations (see Table 6.6). It is particularly notable that at the extremes, for both girls and boys, there is a marked gradient in occupational aspirations across the three groups. At one extreme, the intention to enter a higher status professional occupation is most evident among pupils in group A, and least evident among pupils in group C, with young people in group B occupying an intermediate position. And correspondingly, at the other extreme, mention of lower status semi- and unskilled manual occupations is least likely among pupils in group A, and most likely among pupils in group C, with young people in group B, once more, occupying an intermediate position. Within this overall picture, however, there exist some marked gender differences. These may well be explained by the focus among girls on skilled non-manual occupations (e.g. secretarial and clerical) and among boys on skilled manual occupations (e.g. trades). What is perhaps most notable (and these are pupils' self-reported intentions) is that, within the 'non-academic' group C, the majority of boys hope to enter skilled manual jobs, whilst the largest category of future employment identified by girls in group C is within lower status semi- and unskilled manual jobs. Thus, to summarize, this relatively complex set of findings, pupils in group A aspire to higher-status jobs, pupils in group B occupy an intermediate position, whilst amongst pupils in group C, girls aspire to either junior non-manual positions or to lower-status manual jobs, whereas boys in this third group hope to enter skilled manual jobs or trades. The career aspirations of young people in the three groups are therefore very clearly related to the subject choices made by them in their second year.

Staying-on rates would also appear to be consistent with these variations in occupational intentions among the three groups. As can be seen from Table 6.7, pupils in group A are least likely to consider leaving school early, pupils in group B

Table 6.7: Patterns of subject choice by gender and intention to leave school at the minimum age (third and fourth year pupils in seven local authority secondary schools).
Source: Grampian EO survey, 1994.

Intention to stay on at school beyond 16 years of age	Subject group			All pupils
	Group A	Group B	Group C	
Female				
No (leave)	6%	21%	26%	20%
Undecided	7%	5%	6%	6%
Yes (stay)	87%	74%	68%	74%
Male				
No (leave)	13%	11%	43%	29%
Undecided	6%	7%	9%	7%
Yes (stay)	81%	82%	48%	64%
All pupils	30%	32%	38%	100%

occupy an intermediate position, and pupils in group C are the most likely to see leaving at 16 years of age as a distinct possibility. Once again, there are gender differences within this overall picture, with a greater proportion of girls than boys intending to stay on at school. This is in line with actual patterns of early leaving among girls and boys in Grampian at the present time (see Table 5.5). Further, there are important differences between girls and boys within the three groups (see Table 6.7). Boys from the 'non-academic' group C, for example, are much more likely than other pupils (including girls from the same group) to consider leaving at the minimum age; only a minority of boys in this group state that they intend to stay on at secondary school once they have reached their sixteenth birthday. The situation would therefore appear to be more polarized in the case of boys.

We now draw together our findings for patterns of subject choice, as represented by the three groupings of pupils derived from the cluster analysis. These groups are intended to provide an empirically based description of patterns of choice within the Standard grade curriculum. The findings indicate that there exists a distinctive set of inter-relationships between choice and structural factors, such as gender and social class background, and also between choice and the intended educational and occupational trajectories of pupils. The descriptive labels applied by us to the three groups of pupils would appear to be well justified, with pupils in groups A and B more 'academic' in orientation, and pupils in group C correspondingly less so. What is perhaps most notable in the findings is the marked differences in gender composition of the two 'academic' groups, with group A predominantly 'male' in character and composition, whilst group B is predominantly 'female' in character and composition. It is also notable that pupils in the 'male-academic' group aspire to higher-status occupations than pupils in the corresponding 'female-academic' group. Group C (the 'non-academic' group) would appear at first sight to be less gendered in character, but here our findings clearly highlight significant differences between female and male pupils in this third group with respect to future educational and career aspirations.

Finer-grain gender differences (in terms of social class background and intended educational-occupational trajectories) among the three groups are perhaps best summarized by saying that the situation is more polarized for boys, with the profile of boys within groups A and B fairly similar, but distinctively different from that of boys in group C. There is more of a gradation across the three subject-choice groupings for girls, with girls in groups A and C clearly different, whilst girls in group B occupy an intermediate position between these two extremes. This pattern of gender differences among groups is certainly consistent with a picture where a subgroup of boys – predominantly from manual households – see education as of less relevance, favouring early labour market entry, with the hope of securing employment in higher status manual jobs in the longer run. By contrast, a significant subgroup of girls from manual households intend to stay on at school, but some of these young women would appear to accept that lower status manual occupations may be a possibility, as opposed to secretarial and clerical positions. And among academically oriented pupils in general, those who study a 'male' curriculum (group A) appear to be more ambitious in terms of future aspirations than those who study a 'female' curriculum (group B). Hence, our findings strongly suggest the existence of distinctive gender 'tracks' which are clearly reflected in the subject choices made by young people at 13–14 years of age, and which are also clearly related to their longer-term educational and occupational aspirations. Within these stereotyped patterns of choice, it is evident that only a minority of pupils attempt to 'change track' and to make atypical choices.

Further confirmation of our interpretations of the three subject-choice groupings comes from an examination of pupils' own assessments of academic ability. For the purposes of the survey, a measure of academic self-concept was derived from responses to six questionnaire items, which were

Table 6.8: Variations in academic self-concept with respect to patterns of subject choice and gender (third and fourth year pupils in seven local authority secondary schools).
Source: Grampian EO survey, 1994.

Mean academic self-concept score (standardized z-score)[a]	Subject group			All pupils
	Group A	Group B	Group C	
Female	0.8	0.0	− 0.4	0.0
Male	0.4	0.4	− 0.5	0.0
All pupils	0.5	0.1	− 0.5	0.0

[a] scale derived from 6 Likert type items relating to academic self-concept

modified from an inventory used previously in schools (Youngman, 1979). The six items were used to construct a standardized scale, where positive scores indicated positive assessments of academic ability, and negative scores indicated poorer self-assessments of academic ability. This academic self-concept score is used to explore relative differences between groups of pupils, rather than as an indication of the overall level of ability of a group.

The data presented in Table 6.8 show that pupils in the 'male-academic' group rate their abilities more highly than other pupils in the sample, whilst pupils in the 'non-academic' group are generally more negative in their assessments. These are young people's own assessments of ability, of course, rather than ratings of ability as made by teachers, but such self-perceptions must involve a process of internalizing the messages conveyed by schools. What is more interesting, however, is the existence of gender differences in academic self-concept scores across the three groups (see Table 6.8). Amongst girls, those in the 'male-academic' group (group A) are most positive about their abilities – significantly more so than girls in the 'female-academic' group (group B), with girls in the 'non-academic' group (group C) more negative. By contrast, boys in groups A and B are equally positive about their abilities, whilst boys in group C are generally negative in their assessments.

The attitude of pupils to non-stereotypical subject and career choices was also gauged, in a manner which was similar to that used for academic self-concept. Pupils' responses to six questionnaire items (e.g. 'The school should encourage boys to study subjects usually studied by girls') were used to construct a standardized scale, where these items were modified from part of an inventory used to assess pupils' attitudes to option choice and equal opportunities policies (Pratt *et al.*, 1984). Positive scores on this scale were intended to represent positive attitudes to the encouragement of pupils by schools to consider 'atypical' choices. There is an assumption here that pupils' attitudes run along a continuum, from a perspective which is more challenging of 'conventional' gender-appropriate choices, through to a perspective which is more accepting of the *status quo*. Pupils' attitudes to issues of choice may be much more complex than this simplistic picture suggests, and certainly the responses of some pupils in the survey sample reflected the view that schools should not interfere with the right of individuals to choose as they please. Nevertheless, the data presented in Table 6.9 provide an interesting profile of gender differences across the three subject-choice groupings.

In all three groups, boys would appear to be equally rejecting of the promotion of 'atypical' subject and career choices, whilst girls are apparently more accepting than boys of 'atypical' choice. Girls in group A, who themselves have made clearly non-stereotypical subject choices, are most positive about measures which encourage 'atypical' choice. More surprisingly, the same cannot be said of boys in group B, where the non-stereotypical subject choices made by these boys do not necessarily imply that they feel that such choices should be encouraged by schools more generally. Perhaps boys in group B have particular careers in mind which require that they study what are stereotypically regarded as female subjects, but which are considered by them to be perfectly

111

Table 6.9: Variations in attitude to the promotion of non-stereotyped subject
and career choice with respect to patterns of subject choice and
gender (third and fourth year pupils in seven local authority
secondary schools).
Source: Grampian EO survey, 1994.

Mean EO attitude score (standardized z-score)[a]	Subject group			All pupils
	Group A	Group B	Group C	
Female	0.8	0.4	0.0	0.3
Male	–0.3	–0.3	–0.4	–0.3
All pupils	0.0	0.2	–0.3	0.0

[a] scale derived from 6 Likert type items relating to attitude to promotion
of 'atypical' subject and career choices

'normal' or 'natural' choices given their career intentions, for
example, to train as a chef. It is very notable that there is
little or no evidence in our data to suggest that girls aspire
to becoming builders, electricians, motor mechanics, or
carpenters. Where girls make a-stereotypical subject choices
(group A) the focus is largely on higher education and on
professional careers, and girls in group A are much more
likely to see the challenging of stereotyped gender roles as
important.

The final set of survey results reported in this chapter shifts
the focus away from a consideration of what might be called
'curricular tracks' within the secondary school (as represented
by the three subject-choice groupings of pupils) to a more
detailed examination of influences on pupil choice at the level
of specific Standard grade subjects. Three spheres of influence
are considered here: the self, the family, and the school.
Results for peers are not reported here, since very few pupils
cited friends as a major influence; all schools in the study were
careful to warn pupils against being overly influenced by their
friends. However, follow-up interviews with a sub-sample of
pupils indicate that friends and siblings may be of more
importance than the survey findings might suggest.

Table 6.10: Gender differences in perceptions of self, parents, and school staff (respectively) as having had a major influence on choosing subject, for pupils studying selected Standard grades (third and fourth year pupils in seven local authority secondary schools). *Source:* Grampian EO survey, 1994.

S' grade subject	Perceived as a major influence on choice of subject (%)			S' grade subject	Perceived as a major influence on choice of subject (%)		
	Self	Parents	Staff		Self	Parents	Staff
Office and information studies				*English*			
Female	81%	28%	26%	Female	*All pupils expected*		
Male	72%	37%	17%	Male	*to study English*		
Home economics				*Mathematics*			
Female	84%	24%	16%	Female	*All pupils expected*		
Male	67%	48%	0%	Male	*to study Maths*		
Biology				*Chemistry*			
Female	86%	20%	26%	Female	89%	19%	20%
Male	76%	32%	11%	Male	87%	14%	14%
Music				*Science*			
Female	86%	24%	26%	Female	76%	31%	32%
Male	71%	36%	20%	Male	64%	19%	31%
French				*Geography*			
Female	81%	32%	27%	Female	86%	31%	27%
Male	80%	31%	17%	Male	85%	21%	19%
Modern studies				*Computing*			
Female	85%	34%	28%	Female	86%	22%	21%
Male	86%	31%	21%	Male	85%	20%	20%
History				*Physical education*			
Female	80%	21%	26%	Female	67%	30%	17%
Male	78%	19%	16%	Male	78%	25%	24%
Art				*Physics*			
Female	85%	24%	28%	Female	87%	28%	31%
Male	86%	22%	18%	Male	89%	22%	14%
Social and vocational studies				*Craft and design*			
Female	85%	31%	33%	Female	75%	47%	33%
Male	65%	17%	31%	Male	77%	21%	14%

Table 6.10 lists eighteen subjects within the Standard grade curriculum. These are the same subjects for which gender differences in presentations and attainment at Standard grade were discussed at the end of the previous chapter (see Table 5.7). The subjects run from those where there is a marked

113

over-representation of girls in schools (starting at the top left of the table) through to subjects where there is a marked over-representation of boys (finishing at the bottom right of the table). The perceived importance of self, parents, and staff (respectively) as a major influence on choice is reported only for those pupils who are currently studying the subject. Hence, these data say nothing about the influences that operate on pupils who do *not* study a particular subject.

It is striking how many pupils in the sample cite 'self' as a major influence on choice, right across the range of subjects considered. It would appear that whatever processes are at work, these are effectively internalized by young people. Given the considerable constraints that do in fact operate on subject choice in schools, most pupils do not appear to see themselves as being coerced into making a selection from a limited range of choices. This impression is further reinforced by the many positive responses made to open-ended questions about other subjects that pupils would have liked to study as well as, or instead of, the subjects actually chosen by them.

In the majority of subjects boys and girls were equally likely to feel that their own views were of primary importance when deciding to study a subject. But there are some interesting gender differences within specific subjects. These are: office and information studies, home economics, biology, music, social and vocational studies, general science, and physical education. In all of these subjects (with the notable exception of physical education) girls were more likely than boys to regard themselves as having had a major influence on choosing to study the subject. Physical education is the only subject in the table where boys are more likely than girls to see themselves as a major influence. Four of the subjects where girls are more likely than boys to see themselves as influential are also the four predominantly 'female' subjects in the table (i.e. office and information studies, home economics, biology, and music). And these are the four subjects where boys were more likely than girls to report that their parents had a significant influence; parental influence was seen as more important by girls than boys in all other subjects, although in some instances these differences were small. The remaining three subjects where there was evidence of gender differences in the degree of influence reported by pupils themselves (i.e. social and vocational studies, general science, and physical education) are also those subjects where the picture is different for staff influences. In the great majority of subjects girls are more likely than boys to see staff as influential, but in social and vocational studies, general science, and physical education the relative influence of staff on boys would appear to be greater than in other subjects. Physical education is the one subject where staff influences are significantly greater on boys than girls.

To summarize this rather complex set of results for influences on subject choice, most pupils regard their own views to be of primary importance, whereas the influence of parents and teachers are seen to be of less significance. In most instances, girls are more likely than boys to see parents and teachers as influential. Within this overall picture, however, there are some interesting variations in the relative influence of self, parents, and teachers on girls and boys. In subjects where boys see themselves as having less influence on choice than girls the influence of either parents or teachers on boys is correspondingly raised. Where boys make atypical choices some parents would appear to exert a significant influence on their sons to choose these subjects. This is hardly consistent with the general view that parental attitudes present the major barrier to non-stereotypical subject choice, although exceptional choices may be indicative of exceptional parents. On the other hand, where pupils are perhaps guided by the school to make particular choices on the basis of assessments of ability (e.g. general science) this would appear to be more likely to occur in the case of boys. Finally, physical education is the one subject where girls are clearly less likely than boys to see themselves as influential, and it is the one subject where girls see staff as less influential. Notably, it is also the one Standard grade subject where boys do markedly better than girls in national examinations.

115

The findings from the local study of seven schools in Grampian would therefore suggest that there are very clear curricular 'tracks' among third and fourth year pupils, where these tracks are strongly linked to gender and to (assessments of) ability. Our analysis identifies three broad subject-choice groupings of pupils: there is a 'male-academic' track, a 'female-academic' track, and a 'non-academic' track. The 'non-academic' track is further differentiated along gender lines, much more in terms of furture aspirations, than in terms of overall patterns of subject choice. Only a minority of girls and boys are prepared to shift track, and to make atypical choices. It is interesting that the 'non-academic' curricular track is also not further subdivided into a male and female track in our analysis. This would appear to be because girls and boys in this group tend to study very similar Standard grade subjects across most of the curriculum – due both to practical limitations on choice, and also to the choice of other short courses and modules as alternatives to Standard grades. Hence, the differences in subject choices between girls and boys in the 'non-academic' track are largely focused within technological activities, other short courses and modules, and to a lesser extent within creative and aesthetic activities. Importantly, although these girls and boys study very similar patterns of Standard grade subjects across much of the curriculum, this seems to have little effect on the stark gender divisions in the future aspirations of pupils in the 'non-academic' track.

This is a more general point: it is notable that the differentiation of pupils into three broad subject-choice groups is possible even within a Standard grade curriculum which imposes significant constraints on choice for all pupils. Staff in the seven schools often commented on this during the initial phase of the study when contacts with the schools were first established: 'You'll find that they don't have that much choice when it comes down to it' (Headteacher of urban comprehensive). Nevertheless, our analysis of actual patterns of choice indicates that the choice of Standard grade science subjects *alone* is sufficient to distinguish between almost three-quarters of the pupils in the sample, and in a way that is very clearly structured by a combination of gender and assessments of ability. In broad terms: 40 per cent of the sample are identified as 'non-academic' (with a slightly smaller proportion of girls to boys in this group) with more than 80 per cent of pupils in this group studying general science; 30 per cent of the sample are identified as 'female-academic' (with the proportion of girls to boys at 3 : 1) with around 90 per cent of pupils in the group studying biology; and a further 30 per cent of the sample are identified as 'male-academic' (with the proportion of girls to boys at 1 : 3) with around 95 per cent of pupils in the group studying physics. (Very few pupils in the non-academic group study chemistry, whilst more or less equal numbers of pupils from the two academic groups study chemistry.) Thus, the subject choices made from among physics, chemistry, biology, and general science effectively serve to identify the large majority of pupils as 'non-academic' (general science), 'female-academic' (biology and/or chemistry) or 'male-academic' (physics and/or chemistry), and, as is shown by the results of our analysis, this differentiation between pupils is in terms of scientific subjects, rather than in terms of social and environmental subjects, or in terms of technological activities, or creative and aesthetic activities.

It is perhaps not surprising that the type of scientific subjects studied by pupils in secondary school should serve to highlight gender divisions in patterns of choice so clearly. What might be described as 'positive action' by policy-makers has certainly ensured access to science subjects for all girls: before the implementation of the curriculum framework boys were over-represented in the sciences, with a greater proportion of girls than boys not taking a science subject in third and fourth years of secondary school. Changes in educational policy have therefore ensured that all girls have access to at least one science, but the subjects actually chosen by girls and boys still reflect the gender divisions that were to be found in schools twenty years ago. In practice this means: girls who are 'able' do biology, or perhaps chemistry, but few choose physics; the reverse is true for 'able' boys; and those pupils (girls and boys) who are 'not able' attempt general science. Although the picture has never been as clear-cut as some would suggest, the physical sciences retain high status value in our society, whilst biology as a school subject has had a tradition of being identified with what are perceived as female roles of nurturing and caring. This historical division between school sciences may come to be radically altered with the advent of new technologies, such as bio-engineering and genetics, but at the present time subjects such as physics can still be identified with a dominant culture which has traditionally been viewed as male in its nature and origins. And at the more immediate and practical level, there is the consideration of which science subjects are perceived as most relevant to a career in nursing, or to becoming a motor mechanic.

This brings us full circle in the book, back to historical and cultural perspectives of a woman's place in society (which were first introduced in Chapter 1) and to questions of what is implicitly assumed to be of value in a society which has been largely defined by men, and in which women traditionally have been seen to occupy a subordinate position. One of the key points to be made in Sheila Riddell's (1992) book, *Gender and the Politics of the Curriculum*, is that, in order to assess the extent to which school life reinforces traditional gender divisions, it is necessary to 'critically examine the idea that pupils operate as free agents in selecting their subject options' (p. 3). It is notable that in our study pupils consider themselves to be the principal agents in the process of making choices – not parents, not teachers, and not peers. This would suggest that most pupils claim ownership and responsibility for the choices that *they* have made. But, at the same time, our findings are apparently inconsistent with a picture of pupils as 'free agents' in the selection process, since the findings also clearly show that pupils' patterns of subject choice, where choices exist, are related to structural factors, such as gender and social class background, as well as to assessments and self-perceptions of ability.

Conclusion

This book goes to press twenty years after the Sex Discrimination Act and over two hundred years after Mary Wollstonecraft spelled out the need for changes in girls' education and in society's attitude to women. We have maintained that, despite the availability of her insights for two centuries, a willingness within society to re-examine the role of women was not widespread until the 1970s. Assisted by some powerful new-wave feminist writing, our capacity to profit from such ideas was acquired through the 1960s experience of constantly questioning and re-examining our social and political foundations. But how far has the principled acceptance of equality for women been matched by actual change?

Despite the outlawing of sex discrimination, our evidence shows that traditional patterns of distribution of males and females, both within school and without, have not been radically disturbed. With these patterns still evident, individual pupils and teachers are bound to be affected by resulting perceptions of opportunity.

Wollstonecraft and Mill believed that the prospect of being able to enter a profession would automatically raise the academic attainment of females, and this remains an entirely plausible view. But while entry to the professions is now a realistic goal for many women, *within* professions women still tend to remain in the less senior posts. Access does not produce equality. For women who work in education, obtaining one of the top jobs is unlikely to seem a live option. In common with many professional and managerial occupations, teaching appears to have in place a 'glass ceiling' which women can penetrate only with the greatest difficulty. Conversely, the teaching of younger pupils remains firmly associated with women, reflecting and reinforcing their traditional role as society's carers and nurturers. The few men who would like to teach the youngest groups of schoolchildren experience what we might call a 'glass floor'.

What is the evidence for change (or lack of change) for school pupils? In a speech to heads of independent girls' schools, Gillian Shephard, the then Education Secretary for England and Wales, was reported to have said that:

> Boys could learn a lot from girls, who now out-perform them both at GCSE and A-level ... the balance had at long last been redressed ... But she warned there was now a danger that it would go too far the other way – and asked for ideas on how to raise standards among boys. (TES, 1994)

This statement certainly represents a very positive picture of the current situation for girls in schools, at least in terms of educational achievements; and from a management perspective in which effectiveness is judged on the basis of measurable outcomes, girls clearly do not present a problem. There appears, however, to be a tension between girls' academic performance and research findings which show that girls receive less teacher attention than boys. But such research relies on a very traditional model of teaching and learning and assumes that frequent teacher–pupil interaction is highly desirable. We have suggested that the rise of progressive pedagogy with its emphasis on independent inquiry, group work, and individual study schemes, may have created an environment within which girls can learn more effectively. If this is correct, current political pressure for a return to whole-class teaching should be viewed with concern notwithstanding the underlying desire to raise standards. If there is a problem with standards which has a gender dimension, it would appear to be primarily a problem for boys, and a problem whose roots lie in their socialization. For some boys the role into which they are socialized in our society is at odds with the expectations of school, and the supposed advantages associated with factors such as competitiveness may offer insufficient compensation.

A key question is how far the improvement in girls' academic performance is matched by change in patterns of subject choice. Among the less academically oriented pupils in our study, although girls clearly value education more highly than boys, in broad terms girls and boys study a very similar curriculum. This, however, would appear to have little impact on longer-term career aspirations, which remain strongly demarcated along gender lines.

Among the rest of the pupils in the study, a surprisingly traditional picture emerges, in which choice of scientific subjects represents the most significant form of gender division within the curriculum. If we go back to the eighteenth century, we find Wollstonecraft urging that girls should learn 'the elements of anatomy and medicine'. Significantly for her (generally well justified) reputation as a radical, she invoked women's caring role to explain the aim of such learning: 'not only to enable them to take proper care of their own health, but to make them rational nurses of their infants, parents and husbands' (Wollstonecraft, 1792, p. 298). Remarkably, two hundred years later, biology continues to be the preferred science amongst more able girls.

To make the point more general, our findings show that, among the more academically oriented pupils, where choices are possible, very often girls follow one curriculum and boys follow another. These two separate and gendered curricular tracks are strongly linked to markedly different educational and occupational aspirations for girls and boys. Our concern is that the debate about whether or not girls achieve better overall grades than boys may ultimately be misconceived. In the language of competition and league tables, for much of the time, the great majority of girls and boys may not even be in the same race. And while those girls and boys who are seen to be less able pursue a broadly similar secondary school curriculum, this common experience is not reflected in their differentiated perceptions of their future roles in society.

References

Where two dates appear for the same item, the first indicates the original date of publication, and the second indicates the date of the edition used by the present authors.

Adams, C. (1990), 'Divide and rule: the marriage bar 1918–1945', *in* Paterson, F. and Fewell, J. (eds), *Girls in their Prime: Scottish Education Revisited*, Edinburgh, Scottish Academic Press.

Alexander, R., Rose, J. and Woodhead, C. (1992), *Curriculum Organization and Classroom Practice in Primary Schools*, a discussion paper, London, DES.

Anderson, B. and Zinsser, J. (1990), *A History of their Own: Women in Europe from Pre-history to the Present*, vols 1 and 2, Harmondsworth, Penguin.

Apple, M. (1985), 'Teaching and "women's work": a comparative historical and ideological analysis', *Journal of Education*, **86**, pp. 454–73.

Baker, D. and Jones, D. (1992), 'Opportunity and performance: a sociological explanation for gender differences in academic mathematics', *in* Wrigley, J. (ed.), *Education and Gender Equality*, London, The Falmer Press.

Bergen, B. (1982), 'Only a schoolmaster: gender, class, and the effort to professionalise elementary teaching in England, 1870–1910', *History of Education Quarterly*, **22**, Spring.

Bradley, H. (1989), *Men's Work, Women's Work: A Sociological History of the Sexual Division of Labour in Employment*, Cambridge, Polity Press.

Brophy, J. and Good, T. (1970), 'Teachers' communication of differential expectations', *Journal of Educational Psychology*, **61**, pp. 365–74.

Burton, L. (1993), 'Management, "race" and gender: an unlikely alliance?', *British Educational Research Journal*, **19**, pp. 275–90.

Bynner, J. (1987), 'Coping with transition', *Youth and Policy*, **22**, pp. 25–8.

Byrne, E. (1978), *Women and Education*, London, Tavistock.

Casey, K. and Apple, M. (1989), 'Gender and the conditions of teachers' work', *in* Acker, S. (ed.), *Teachers, Gender and Careers*, London, Falmer Press.

Corr, H. (1983), 'The sexual division of labour in the Scottish teaching profession, 1872–1914', *in* Humes, W. and Paterson, H. (eds), *Scottish Culture and Scottish Education 1800–1980*, Edinburgh, John Donald.

Cox, C. B. and Dyson, A. (eds) (1969), *Fight for Education: A Black Paper*, London, Critical Quarterly Society.

Crowther Committee (1959), *15 to 18*, a report of the Central Advisory Council for Education (England), London, Ministry of Education.

Croxford, L. (1994), 'Equal opportunities in the secondary school curriculum in Scotland, 1977–1991', *British Educational Research Journal*, 20, pp. 371–91.

Cunnison, S. (1989), 'Gender joking in the staffroom', *in* Acker, S. (ed.), *Teachers, Gender and Careers*, London, Falmer Press.

Darling, J. and Glendinning, A. (1993), *Equal Opportunities: School Staffing*, a research report prepared for Grampian Region, Aberdeen, Grampian Regional Council.

Dearden, R. F. (1968), *The Philosophy of Primary Education*, London, Routledge and Kegan Paul.

Delamont, S. (1984), 'Sex roles and schooling', *Journal of Adolescence*, 7, pp. 329–36.

Department for Education (1993a), *Women in Post-Compulsory Education*, London, HMSO.

Department for Education (1993b), *Statistics of Education: Teachers in Service, England and Wales 1991*, London, HMSO.

Department for Education (1994a), *GCSE and GCE A/AS Examination Results 1992/93*, London, HMSO.

Department for Education (1994b), *GCSE and GCE A/AS Level Performance of Candidates Attempting Two or More GCE A/AS Levels*, London, HMSO.

Department for Education (1994c), *Statistics of Education: Public Examinations, GCSE and GCE 1993*, London, HMSO.

Dex, S. (1987), *Women's Occupational Mobility*, London, Macmillan.

Douglas-Hamilton, Lord J. (1993), reported in *The Scotsman*, 16 November.

Equal Opportunities Commission (1993), *Women and Men in Britain 1993*, London, HMSO.

Etzioni, A. (1969), *The Semi-Professions and their Organization*, New York, The Free Press.

Evetts, J. (1990), *Women in Primary Teaching*, London, Unwin Hyman.

Firestone, S. (1970)(1972), *The Dialectic of Sex*, London, Paladin.

Floud, J. and Scott, W. (1961), 'Recruitment to teaching in England and Wales', *in* Halsey *et al*. (eds), *Education, Economy and Society*, New York, The Free Press.

Floud, J., Halsey, A. H. and Martin, F. (1956), *Social Class and Educational Opportunity*, London, Heinemann.

Fordyce, J. (1765)(1766), *Sermons to Young Women*, London: printed for A. Millar *et al*.

French, J. and French, P. (1984), 'Gender imbalances in the primary classroom', *Educational Research*, 26, pp. 127–36.

Friedan, B. (1963)(1965), *The Feminine Mystique*, Harmondsworth, Penguin.

Gerver, E. and Hart, L. (1991), *Strategic Women: How do they Manage in Scotland?*, Aberdeen, Aberdeen University Press.

Grant, R. (1989), 'Heading for the top – the career experiences of a group of women deputies in one LEA', *Gender and Education*, 1, pp. 13–25.

Grassick, M. (1993), quoted in *Scottish Business Insider*, May.

Greer, G., (1970), *The Female Eunuch*, London, Paladin.

Gregory, J. (1774)(1808), *A Father's Legacy to his Daughters*, London, Cadell & Davis.

Halsey, A. H., Floud, J. and Anderson, C. A. (1961), *Education, Economy and Society*, New York, The Free Press.

Hendry, L. B., Shucksmith, J., Love, J. and Glendinning, A. (1993), *Young People's Leisure and Lifestyles*, London, Routledge.

Hill, T. (1994), 'Primary headteachers' careers: a survey of primary school heads with particular reference to women's career trajectories', *British Educational Research Journal*, 20, pp. 197–207.

HMI (1975), *Differences of Provision for Boys and Girls in Scottish Secondary Schools*, Edinburgh, Scottish Education Department.

Kelly, A. (1988), 'Gender differences in teacher–pupil interactions: a meta-analytic review', *Research in Education*, 39, pp. 1–23.

Lawton, D. (1977), *Education and Social Justice*, London, Sage.

Levin, B. (1970), *The Pendulum Years: Britain and the Sixties*, London, Pan Books.

Lobban, G. (1974), 'Sex roles in reading schemes', *in* Weiner, G. and Arnot, M. (eds) (1987), *Gender under Scrutiny*, London, Hutchinson.

MacIntosh, M. (1990), '"Caught between the two": gender and race in a Scottish school', *in* Paterson, F. and Fewell, J. (eds), *Girls in their Prime: Scottish Education Revisited*, Edinburgh, Scottish Academic Press.

Marshall, C. (1985), 'From culturally defined to self-defined: career stages of women administrators', *Journal of Educational Thought*, 19, pp. 134–47

Merrett, F. and Wheldall, K. (1992), 'Teachers' use of praise and reprimands to boys and girls', *Educational Review*, 44, pp. 73–9.

Middleton, S. (1989), 'Educating feminists: a life-history study', *in* Acker, S. (ed.), *Teachers, Gender and Careers*, London, Falmer Press.

Mill, J. S. (1869)(1986), *The Subjection of Women*, Buffalo, Prometheus Books.

Millett, K. (1970)(1971), *Sexual Politics*, London, Rupert Hart-Davis.

National Union of Teachers (1980), *Promotion and the Woman Teacher*, London, NUT/EOC.

Neill, A. S. (1968), *Summerhill*. Harmondsworth, Penguin.

Newsom Committee (1963), *Half Our Future*, a report of the Central Advisory Council for Education (England), London, Ministry of Education.

Nisbet, J. (1975), 'Innovation – bandwagon or hearse?', *in* Harris, A. *et al.* (eds), *Curriculum Innovation*, London, Croom Helm.

Oram, A. (1989), 'A master should not serve under a mistress: women and men teachers 1900–1970', *in* Acker, S. (ed.), *Teachers, Gender and Careers*, London, Falmer Press.

Parsons, J., Kaczala, C. and Meece, J. (1982), 'Socialization of achievement, attitudes and beliefs: classroom influences', *Child Development*, 53, pp. 310–21.

Plowden Committee (1967), *Children and their Primary Schools*, a Report of the Central Advisory Council for Education (England), London, DES.

Powney, J. and Weiner, G. (1992), *'Outside of the Norm': Equity and Management in Educational Institutions'*, revised edition, London, South Bank University.

Pratt, J., Bloomfield, J. and Seale, C. (1984), *Option Choice: A Question of Equal Opportunity*, Windsor, NFER-Nelson.

Purvis, J. (1991), *A History of Women's Education in England*, Milton Keynes, Open University Press.

Riddell, S. (1992), *Gender and the Politics of the Curriculum*, London, Routledge.

Robbins Committee (1963), *Higher Education*, London, HMSO.

Robinson, J. (1963), *Honest to God*, London, Student Christian Movement.

Rousseau, J.-J. (1762)(1974), *Emile*, London, Dent.

Scottish Education Department (1965), *Primary Education in Scotland* (the 'Primary Memorandum'), Edinburgh, HMSO.

Scottish Education Department (1983), *The Munn and Dunning Reports: Implementation of the Government's Proposals*, Edinburgh, HMSO.

Scottish Education Department (1989), *The Teaching of Languages other than English in Scottish Schools*, Edinburgh, HMSO.

Scottish Examination Board (1993), *Report for 1992*, Dalkeith, SEB.

Scottish Examination Board (1995), *Gender and SCE Examinations*, SEB Research Bulletin 3, Dalkeith, SEB.

Scottish Office Education Department (1992), *Scottish Teachers: Gender, Promoted Posts and Other Issues*, September 1990, Edinburgh, HMSO.

Short, C. (1991), *Dear Clare: This is What Women Feel about Page 3*, London, Hutchinson.

Sikes, P., Measor, L. and Woods, P. (1985), *Teacher Careers: Crises and Continuities*, London, Falmer Press.

Simpson, R. L. and Simpson, I. H. (1969), 'Women and bureaucracy in the semi-professions', *in* Etzioni, A. (ed.), *The Semi-Professions and their Organization*, New York, Free Press.

Spender, D. (1985), *For the Record: The Making and Meaning of Feminist Knowledge*, London, Women's Press.

Stanworth, M. (1981), *Gender and Schooling*, London, Hutchinson.

Stirner, M. (1842)(1967), *The False Principle of Our Education*, translated by Robert Beebe, Colorado Springs, Ralph Myles.

Strathclyde Department of Education (1988), *Sex Equality in the Education Service*, Glasgow, Strathclyde Regional Council.

Sutherland, M. (1981), *Sex Bias in Education*, Oxford, Basil Blackwell.

TES (1994), 'Girls urged to set boys an example', *Times Educational Supplement*, 12 November.

Waller, W. (1932), *The Sociology of Teaching*, New York, Wiley.

Wollstonecraft, M. (1792)(1975), *A Vindication of the Rights of Woman*, Harmondsworth, Penguin.

Youngman, M. (1979), *Analysing Social and Educational Research Data*, London, McGraw-Hill.

Name Index

Subject Index